THE MATURE MANAGER
Managing from Inside Out

D1394498

Over 160,000 copies of Tony Humphreys' books have already sold in the English language. Currently there are twenty-four foreign translations.

Books by Tony Humphreys
All About Children
A Different Kind of Discipline
A Different Kind of Teacher
Leaving the Nest: What Families are all About
Myself, My Partner
The Power of 'Negative' Thinking
Self-Esteem: The Key to Your Child's Future
Whose Life Are You Living?
Work and Worth
Children Feeling Good (Veritas)

Audio Tapes and CDs by Tony Humphreys
Self-Esteem for Adults
Raising Your Child's Self Esteem
Work and Self
Embrace Failure (Veritas)

THE MATURE MANAGER
MANAGING FROM INSIDE OUT

Tony Humphreys
BA, HDE, MA, PhD

Newleaf

£71.00

**To all those who aspire
to true leadership**

H 1 6 7, 138

658
001

Newleaf
Gill & Macmillan Ltd
Hume Avenue
Park West
Dublin 12
with associated companies throughout the world
www.gillmacmillan.ie

© 2006 Tony Humphreys

ISBN-13: 978 0 7171 4000 8
ISBN-10: 0 7171 4000 8

Print origination by
Carrigboy Typesetting Services, Co. Cork
Printed by ColourBooks Ltd, Dublin

*The paper used in this book is made from the wood pulp of
managed forests. For every tree felled, at least one tree is
planted, thereby renewing natural resources.*

A catalogue record is available for this book
from the British Library.

1 3 5 4 2

CONTENTS

CHAPTER 1

A DIFFERENT KIND OF MANAGER

The impetus to write this book came from many years of giving staff development seminars and workshops within diverse work organisations. Topics covered included: Stress Management, Effective Communication, Managing Self-Esteem, Conflict-Resolution, Effective Management and Emotion and Motivation. Work with individual managers who came for one-to-one help underpins many of the insights offered. Furthermore, managing staff in business ventures of my own provided experiences that inform the writing of this book. Of course earlier experiences of being employed in a non-managerial and managerial capacity in business, educational and health organisations also contributed to the ideas presented.

The broad focus of the book is on the interior world of the manager and how it influences his interactions with others, particularly his managerial style. There is no manager (or employee) who does not carry emotional baggage into the workplace. It is the resolution of a poor sense of self and inner conflicts that creates the positive mind-set for mature and effective management. This book is not about management strategies and techniques because it is my belief and observation that such approaches are not fully effective unless they spring from the manager's solid and wise interiority. The book is primarily about managers managing their interior world so that they approach their managerial tasks in the most enlightened and productive way.

A very definite aim of the book is to develop an understanding of what happens within managers and between managers and other employees. A further goal is to help managers, from a position of being able to understand their own inner and outer responses, to be better able to understand and respond maturely to the challenging behaviours of employees. The book will also show that a manager who possesses a deep understanding of human behaviour is in a powerful position to enhance relationships with employees and increase their motivation and commitment to work.

The understanding of human behaviour that is presented is an evolution of that outlined in previous books of mine, particularly *The Power of 'Negative' Thinking, Work and Worth, Take Back Your Life* and *Whose Life Are You Living?* The essential message is that all human behaviour makes sense, no matter how effective, difficult or despicable. Clinical experience has shown me that all our behaviours have been shaped by our earlier experiences and can be exacerbated by current experiences; such exacerbation can continue until a person has learned to know self and separate out that inner core from the responses of others. It is with the defensive responses of self and employees that managers are especially challenged. In order to effect change, the understanding of these defensive responses (for example, aggression, irresponsibility, passivity, poor motivation, non-cooperation) is critical. The task of the manager is to get behind the defensive responses and focus on what lies hidden. More often than not, what are being masked are issues of low self-esteem.

However, in understanding such behaviours there is no attempt to dilute the nature, and the impact on self and others, of difficult human responses. On the contrary, it is only by calling a spade a spade that real progress can be made in determining the whys and wherefores of human reactions. Nevertheless, the interpretations shown are non-judgemental and empathic; if such was not the case then understanding would be threatening rather than enlightening in nature. It is my expectation (and belief) that through the incorporation and application of my approach to the complex and responsible task of management, managers will reach a greater realisation of their own and their employees' potential. Such a development greatly benefits the work organisation that embraces the mature management of its people.

In writing this book, the readership I had in mind were all those who are in managerial positions, whether in industry (either service or manufacturing), education, sport, professional or social services — indeed for all those who find themselves with responsibility for managing, or with a leadership role, in any organisation whether large or small.

What can managers gain from reading (and re-reading) this book?

- ☐ the means of evaluating their own sense of self and how this influences their management style
- ☐ the understanding that management is predominantly about enhancing relationships with self and with employees
- ☐ the appreciation that the enabling of employees is central to managing
- ☐ the ability to identify their style of management and, where necessary, to change to a more mature style
- ☐ the knowledge that all communication starts with and is about self
- ☐ the skills to distinguish between open and defensive communication and how to communicate from the inside out
- ☐ the appreciation that conflict provides the opportunity to deepen relationships within and without and to progress the aims of the work organisation

☐ the awareness of what organisational support is required for effective inside-out management.

The book invites readers to evaluate where they are at in terms of knowing self/not knowing self, knowing employees/not knowing employees, managing from a mature inner place/managing from a place of defensiveness, exercising open communication/exercising defensive communication, viewing conflict as an opportunity/ viewing conflict as a threat, engaging in mature conflict-resolution/ engaging in defensive conflict-resolution.

The expectation is that most managers will detect that they have some mature qualities but also defensive qualities that arise from their own emotional baggage. The challenge is to capitalise on the mature qualities and to understand and free themselves of those aspects of self that block personal, interpersonal and professional development.

It is the responsibility of each of us to reflect on how we are within ourselves and how we relate to others. The welfare of society is dependent on such a review process. It is important that society creates the opportunities and the support for this mature accountability. For those in positions of leadership, the need to reflect daily is even more urgent since the influence wielded can have lasting effects on the well-being and potential of others. It is vital that work organisations, regardless of size, provide the structures and positive climate for this review process and engage in examining its own processes.

The book will certainly challenge managers, but in a way that is non-judgemental, empathic and encouraging; an approach that the reader also needs to adopt. The aim of the book is to engage the reader in a personal and interpersonal reflective process. This process may well give rise to fear, but persistence will reap considerable rewards in terms of personal and professional fulfilment, satisfaction and effectiveness.

Finally, while the manager is referred to in the masculine gender, this is merely to avoid the more extreme examples of inclusive language. Women are increasingly filling managerial roles, and are bringing much-needed qualities to the workplace. I hope no one will feel excluded by the limitations of simple usage of the English language!

CHAPTER 2

MANAGERS WHO KNOW THEMSELVES

KNOWING SELF

The Chinese philosopher Lao Tzu said that 'to know others is learned, to know self is wise'. It is a requirement of all psychotherapists and psychoanalysts to know themselves in order to ensure, as much as is possible, that they do not project their problems on to their clients and do not take on their clients' difficulties as if they were their own. There has been an unprecedented rise in the number of individuals, couples and families seeking psycho-social help for their problems in living. Many organisations are now making confidential counselling available to those employees who present with problems in the workplace. Currently, bullying and addiction to alcohol are the more common problems for which help is sought for managers and other employees. The problem with this trend is that the work of knowing self is called for 'after the horse has bolted'. It is regrettable that managers or workers have to manifest problems that are highly visible and that pose a serious block to the well-being of others and to productivity *before* help is sought.

No one is without vulnerabilities and defensive screens; it needs to become an integral part of our living that we reflect regularly on how we are with ourselves and with others. More especially, those individuals who hold positions of power and influence — parents, teachers, clergy, child-minders, community leaders, all the caring professions, entrepreneurs, managers, supervisors and politicians – have an urgent responsibility to take on the life-long task of knowing self. Knowing self is the most important work of all and the process is best begun in our earliest years within homes, schools, churches and communities.

As for adults, the process of knowing self is not easy and, accordingly, it tends to be the road less travelled. When you are surrounded by company owners, other managers and workers who operate from a position of defence, it takes huge strength and support from others to go against the oppressive tide. The catch-cries within many organisations are: 'don't question the top people', 'keep a low profile', 'don't ruffle feathers' and 'let sleeping dogs lie'. The belief is, and for good reason, that 'if you raise your head above the parapet, you'll have it shot off'. Unless the ethos of a workplace creates a safe environment wherein realness, assertion of needs and rights, authenticity and support for the personal realisation of potential are encouraged and supported, it is difficult for managers or employees to take up the essential challenge of knowing self. Nonetheless, individual managers cannot afford to wait for the organisation to transform itself into a more enlightened body before starting the life-enhancing process of freeing oneself from insecurities, fears and vulnerabilities.

The process of knowing self is four-fold:

- ☐ Identify in what ways you are real
- ☐ Identify in what ways you are protective
- ☐ Realise what aspects of self lie hidden behind your protectors
- ☐ Begin to actualise what lies hidden (living from the inside out).

IDENTIFYING IN WHAT WAYS YOU ARE REAL

Many individuals appear to have a lot more difficulty in identifying their 'positive' compared to their 'negative' qualities. As for all behaviour, there is a wisdom to this reticence. Being real and authentic can be most threatening when you are faced with highly defensive behaviour on the part of others. Reflect on when you were a child; to what degree, if any, could you assert what was true and real about you to your parents, teachers, clergy, relatives or other significant adults? Here and now, in the workplace, to what extent do you feel it is safe for you to express what is real to those who hold the decision-making power within the organisation? Reflection shows why it is not surprising that individuals fight shy of acknowledging their positive qualities. There is a lot more support and reinforcement for saying what people in their defensiveness want to hear, rather than saying what is real. In all sorts of systems, including workplaces, co-dependence is much more common than independence.

Success is probably the most appreciated behaviour in the workplace, but such exclusive emphasis engenders a dependence on success and a consequent fear of failure. Performance anxiety is the most common anxiety to be found in the workplace and considerably reduces effectiveness. Organisations would be better served by encouraging and praising realness, authenticity, the assertion of rights and needs, identification of any neglect experienced, risk-taking, a challenging of the organisation's values, traditions, management style, a willingness to put forward different ways of doing things and having a balanced lifestyle.

Whether or not the work organisation supports one being oneself, being real and genuine, managers, for their own sakes, as well as for the welfare of those colleagues who have a reporting relationship to them, need to know and acknowledge their mature qualities so that they can capitalise on these true aspects of self in their management role. Below is a list of some of the mature qualities that are essential, not only to effective management, but also to a fulfilling life; these qualities are noted as being head (masculine) or heart (feminine) or combined head and heart qualities. The more of the qualities you recognise in yourself, the greater the maturity present.

WAYS OF BEING MATURE

☐ authentic (m)	☐ adventurous (m)
☐ genuine (m)	☐ open (m,f)
☐ sincere (f)	☐ flexible (m)
☐ respectful (f)	☐ sociable (m)
☐ equal (m)	☐ understanding (m,f)
☐ definite (m)	☐ fair (m)
☐ congruent (m,f)	☐ considerate (f)
☐ radical (m)	☐ caring (f)
☐ different (m)	☐ inclusive (f)
☐ assertive (m)	☐ spiritual (f)
☐ ambitious (m)	☐ approachable (m,f)
☐ proactive (m)	☐ supportive (f)
☐ empathic (f)	☐ emotionally expressive (f)
☐ appreciative (f)	☐ independent (m,f)
☐ creative (m,f)	☐ decisive (m)
☐ confident (m,f)	☐ challenging (m)
☐ self-possessed (m,f)	☐ available (m,f)
☐ dynamic (m)	☐ unconditionally valuing (m,f)
☐ fearless (m,f)	☐ apologetic when wrong (m,f)
☐ humorous	☐ personally friendly (m,f)
☐ balanced in lifestyle (m,f)	

Experience shows that male managers are unlikely to have had opportunities to bring forward many of the heart qualities, focusing instead on the head qualities. On the other hand, female managers will be more likely to have the safety to openly express many of the heart behaviours listed, but perhaps not too many of the head qualities. Of course, this is not a hard and fast situation because there are men who possess more of the heart qualities than the head ones and, likewise, there are women who possess more head than heart qualities. But the reality is that (though some change is certainly afoot) the socialisation of children has polarised and continues to polarise males and females in terms of exposure to certain human qualities. Systematic observation has shown that mothers, who still do 90 per cent of the parenting, unwittingly steer their male children away from the 'heart' requirements within the family and direct them towards the outward/head domain of family living. These mothers tend to do the converse for their female offspring.

Up to recent times, men have accepted this situation, but there is a growing male movement demanding the right to equal parenting and to be given opportunities to develop their heart/ feminine side. Women have been quicker — through the feminist movement of the last several decades — to seek expression of head qualities such as assertion, ambition, dynamism, drive, determination, definiteness, leadership, entrepreneurship, inventiveness and industry.

All managers have a responsibility to evaluate their level of maturity and to determine which of the above-listed qualities they possess and which ones are not part of their behavioural repertoire. Where there is significant absence of mature qualities, it is incumbent on the individual manager to correct the situation. It is equally important that the organisation he works for ensures that he possesses these necessary human qualities and, where there is a deficit, provides opportunities for the manager to correct the imbalance.

IDENTIFYING IN WHAT WAYS YOU ARE PROTECTIVE

Facing your protective behaviours may be the hardest step of all, not least because many of our protectors are subconscious, but also because we are adept at rationalising those defensive behaviours that are clearly distressing to self or others. Be encouraged by the fact that, since you have continued to read this book up to this point, there must be a certain readiness in you to begin to consciously examine your protectors. If you have already found this book highly threatening to your defensive position, then you may need to find support in order to continue reading it.

The purpose of reflecting on your defences is threefold: so that you may come to realise that your defensive behaviours are your allies; so that you may come to see that they are 100 per cent about your vulnerability, and that they can act like blows to the presence of those in your charge; and so that you may come to know that the opposite of your defensive response is the aspect of self that is hidden and needs to be brought into the light.

In order to assist you in your reflection, a list of the more common defensive behaviours is set out below. These defences can be categorised as being of an intrapersonal or interpersonal nature; here, these two main categories are further set out under the headings 'passive', 'aggressive' and 'passive-aggressive'. Whilst the intrapersonal defences appear to be more threatening to the manager's own self they also represent a threat to others. The interpersonal defences are much more obviously a threat to the psycho-social welfare of others but, of course, they are also a block to the manager's own psycho-social well-being.

Intrapersonal ways of being defensive
PASSIVE PROTECTORS

☐ not-listening to self	☐ alcohol dependent
☐ lack of emotion	☐ pessimistic
☐ denial	☐ anxious about self
☐ lack of ambition	☐ hypochondriacal
☐ lack of self-care	☐ fatalistic
☐ ashamed of self	

AGGRESSIVE PROTECTORS

☐ highly critical of self	☐ berates self
☐ self-mutilates	☐ hates self
☐ negatively labels self	

PASSIVE-AGGRESSIVE PROTECTORS

☐ drug dependent	☐ suicidal
☐ anorexic	☐ obsessive-compulsive
☐ bulimic	

Interpersonal ways of being defensive
PASSIVE PROTECTORS

☐ conformity	☐ timidity
☐ avoidance of risk-taking	☐ personalising
☐ helplessness	☐ not listening
☐ emotional withdrawal	☐ rustout (loss of motivation)
☐ hypersensitivity to criticism	☐ fearfulness
☐ physical withdrawal	☐ sulkiness
☐ over-pleasing of others	☐ avoidance of social contact
☐ shyness	☐ long hours of work

→

PASSIVE PROTECTORS (CONT.)

- ☐ choking back upset
- ☐ bottling up feelings
- ☐ perfectionism
- ☐ worrying unduly
- ☐ verbal withdrawal
- ☐ dependent
- ☐ suppression of feelings/needs
- ☐ depression
- ☐ living through others

AGGRESSIVE PROTECTORS

- ☐ verbally harassing
- ☐ taunting
- ☐ ridiculing
- ☐ bullying
- ☐ 'negatively' labelling
- ☐ being cynical
- ☐ being sarcastic
- ☐ denigrading
- ☐ being controlling
- ☐ being vindictive
- ☐ rebelling
- ☐ having temper tantrums
- ☐ shouting
- ☐ showing hostile humour
- ☐ humiliating others
- ☐ embarrassing others
- ☐ being judgemental
- ☐ being dominant
- ☐ comparing
- ☐ being superior
- ☐ being fiercely competitive
- ☐ blaming
- ☐ being dismissive
- ☐ being highly critical
- ☐ having unreal expectations

PASSIVE-AGGRESSIVE PROTECTORS

- ☐ gossiping
- ☐ complaining
- ☐ being sick
- ☐ working less
- ☐ showing burnout
- ☐ displaying psychosomatic complaints
- ☐ ignoring inefficiency
- ☐ being absent

There tend to be many more interpersonal than intrapersonal defences; the reason for this is that there is a much greater need to defend oneself against the slings and arrows of the active defensive responses of others, particularly the significant others in our lives. Intrapersonal protectors are more of a response to neglectful behaviours that are passive in nature, such as the absence of affection, the existence of depression, lack of nurturing, lack of affirmation, lack of emotional expression, timidity, high anxiety, helplessness, conformity, non-listening, lack of encouragement, lack of ambition.

Whether a defensive behaviour is intrapersonal or interpersonal, passive or active in nature, the persons at the receiving end of such protective responses are likely to feel the need, in turn, to defend themselves, unless they are mature enough to be able to stay separate from others' defensive responses.

When noticing the defensive behaviours that are part of your way of relating to others, it is important to consider how frequently you engage in these behaviours, how intense they are, their duration when manifested, and how long these protectors have been in place. The intensity of a defensive response can vary from mild to very intense; for example, you may become mildly aggressive (complaining, being somewhat cross in your tone of voice, impatient, annoyed) or you may be grossly aggressive (shouting, humiliating the person, labelling, being threatening). How often defensive behaviours occur is a critical consideration because it is very threatening for anyone to experience in any one day several expressions of another's defensive behaviours. Furthermore, the duration of the difficult behaviour is an indication of its likely impact. How long defensive behaviours last over time is a crucial consideration. I have come across many individuals who have experienced long-term (anything from one to twenty years) neglect at the hands of a manager.

PROTECTORS AS ALLIES

Accepting that your protectors are your allies can be a difficult concept, particularly when defensive responses, such as violence towards self or aggression towards others, are so obviously a major source of threat. However, the psychological truth is that you would not engage in a defensive response unless there was something to protect and that something is some particular aspect of self that, up to this point, you have dared not reveal. It takes some of the sting out of your defensive behaviours — whether they be interpersonal or intrapersonal in nature — when you realise that they are clever attempts to offset threats to your psycho-social well-being. But, alongside that understanding, there is the painful reality that your protective ways can lessen, demean, belittle, invalidate and be dismissive of the presence of another person.

Taking account of the hurt caused is necessary if you are truly serious about knowing self. Notice the phrase 'taking account of', rather than 'taking responsibility for'. In my experience, the latter is judgemental in nature and assumes that the person has deliberately and coldly set out to demean another. This assumption is not accurate; the intention is not to hurt but to protect self and if the manager were in a place of peace with self, he would not act in this way. When we are confronting a defensive behaviour in ourselves or in someone else which threatens the presence of others, we need to hold in balance both the psychological reality of the hurt that lies within the person who is being defensive and the social reality of the hurt that lies without in the person at the receiving end of the defensive behaviour. The phrase 'taking account of' holds both realities. There is no intention to blame or judge, but there is a clear assertion of the need for the person who perpetrates behaviour that lessens the presence of another to own, take responsibility, apologise for and correct these defensive ways.

Defences, then, are allies against threat; they are sentinels, guardians of your sacred and unique self. Alongside that truth, they are also threats to the sacred presence of another. In understanding the coexistence of these two truths you are ready to progress to the next step, whereby you begin to see how each one of your defences points directly to that aspect of self which is repressed or suppressed and needs to be brought into the open.

PROTECTORS AS MIRRORS OF WHAT LIES HIDDEN

Ask yourself the question: 'If I tend to be dominating and aggressive, what aspects of self are these two defences hiding and what would I be fearful or terrified of showing?' It seems to me the answer is concerned with being in charge of my own life and being assertive about my own rights and needs. When you look closely at your discovery of those aspects of self which you have recovered, you can see that they are directly opposite to the defensive responses you regularly practised. It is the ingenuity of defensive behaviours that, while they effectively mask those aspects of self that circumstances have forced you to repress or suppress, at the same time they mirror what you have hidden and need now to reveal.

Whether the defences, then, are of an intrapersonal or inter-personal nature, whether they are passive, aggressive or passive-aggressive, they point to the necessity for the opposite behaviour to be recovered from repression or suppression. Your defences provide the opportunities for seeing what is hidden and progressing to a freer place of living.

The examples below are presented to help you reflect upon what hidden aspect of self is mirrored in different types of defensive behaviour you may have identified as being part of your behavioural repertoire.

What lies behind common defences

THE DEFENCE	THE HIDDEN ASPECT OF SELF THAT NEEDS EXPRESSION
☐ blaming others	☐ be responsible for self
☐ being cynical and sarcastic	☐ say what you really think and feel
☐ being depressed	☐ live your own life
☐ being emotionless	☐ be expressive and receptive to all emotions
☐ being a perfectionist	☐ embrace failure
☐ being critical of self	☐ assert the separateness of self from your behaviour
☐ being hypersensitive to criticism	☐ think well of self
☐ lacking ambition	☐ rediscover the adventure of life
☐ being possessive of others	☐ possess self
☐ being hostile	☐ reach out to others
☐ being conformist	☐ live your own life
☐ being indecisive	☐ take risks
☐ being highly anxious	☐ affirm self
☐ being vindictive	☐ take responsibility for your own feelings of hurt
☐ being neglectful of self	☐ know you deserve to take care of self
☐ being ruthless	☐ find the solid ground of self
☐ being suicidal	☐ break the silence on hidden neglect
☐ being paranoid	☐ trust your own intuition
☐ showing obsessive-compulsive behaviour	☐ express the separateness of your self from your behaviour
☐ being a workaholic	☐ work on self-development
☐ being rigid and inflexible	☐ celebrate difference

DETECTING WHAT IS MISSING

Another way of realising your array of defences is to reflect on
what ought to be in your repertoire of behaviours, but is not there.
As young children we tend to display the full breadth of what it
means to be human; exhibiting both our masculine and our
feminine qualities. Regrettably, as young children we begin to
encounter the threats to being self that arise from the defensive
behaviours of parents, other significant adults, and siblings, and
quickly begin to repress or suppress those qualities of self that
have come under threat.

The typical natural responses of young children are:

☐ Receptivity to nurturing   ☐ Calmness
☐ Expression of all feelings   ☐ Humour
☐ Curiosity   ☐ Peacefulness
☐ Excitement   ☐ Risk-taking
☐ Eagerness to learn   ☐ Freshness
☐ High energy   ☐ Expansiveness
☐ Spontaneity   ☐ Spaciousness
☐ Adventuresomeness   ☐ Alertness
☐ Openness to failure   ☐ Intelligence
☐ Not attached to success   ☐ Joyfulness
☐ Natural   ☐ Motivation
☐ Free of having to prove self   ☐ Creativity
☐ Gentleness   ☐ Inventiveness

In reflecting on this list of behaviours, you will notice there are
some that you now have no hesitancy in displaying (✓), and others
that you either have difficulty in expressing or that are just not in
your repertoire (*). Your reflection may bring back memories of the
hurtful experiences that caused you to bury or dilute certain
personal qualities. As best you can, stay with the feelings that arise

– sadness, grief, anger, rage, anxiety, fear – and comfort yourself, as you would want to comfort a child. These feelings – referred to as emergency feelings – are both requesting you to attend to the hurts you have experienced, and also inviting you to free yourself of early experiences and begin to express what you were forced to repress or suppress.

Another experience your reflection might give rise to is that you may begin to recognise the defensive behaviours you created to ensure you would not inadvertently express the taboo qualities. Working with the defensive behaviours that have come to your attention, and using the list above as your guide, see if you can discover the opposite desirable quality that lies hidden behind each of your protectors. This process of developing a defensive behaviour that is directly opposite to the desirable hidden quality is known as *reaction formation* and it happens quite subconsciously.

LIVING FROM THE INSIDE OUT

The manager who lives his life from the inside out takes his cues from within and acts out from his own knowledge of self, his belief and his values. He tends to be non-conformist, but strongly co-operative. He is conscious of the need to balance his time, energy, resources and commitment among his own self, his partner, his children, his workplace and his friends. He communicates from an 'I' position; is an active listener. Conflict is embraced as an opportunity to deepen relationships and to improve creativity and productivity. Disrespect of himself or others is not tolerated. This manager is unconditional in his regard for others, empathic and genuine in his responses.

Of course, no manager is going to possess all the desirable qualities listed above. Neither is anyone going to be real and authentic in all his interactions; there will be times when he slips back into being defensive. However, the difference between the manager who does not know self and the manager who knows self is that the latter will notice when he acts out from the solid place of self (inside-out) and when he reacts defensively (outside-in). His defensive responses will cue him to reflect on his behaviour and to detect what needs to be seen. Little difficulty will be seen in his admitting that he was mistaken or had acted out of line; readiness to apologise and to follow through in action is shown. He understands, too, that when individual employees have felt harassed, marginalised, 'put down' or humiliated, they may not initially be open to his apology and he can allow them time to heal the hurt experienced. He knows that he will eventually convince them of his sincerity in his mature interactions with them.

This manager will also analyse *what* were the circumstances that gave rise to his defensive response, *with whom* did it occur, *where* did it occur, *when* did it happen and, most of all, *why* did he resort to a protective response. Each of these enquiries will provide him with the information he requires to put him back on the track of nurturance and the enablement of employees. For example, the *what* may have been a budget meeting, the *with whom* may have been a particular person within the group, the *where* may have been in the boardroom and the *when* 5 p.m. Friday afternoon. The *why* will not be as readily visible, but reflection may bring attention to, for example, not feeling comfortable with budget meetings because of a lack of confidence and mathematical competence and a fear of being exposed. The particular person he reacted to may be the one person at the meeting who might spot his 'weakness'. The *where* may not have been a contributing factor, but the Friday afternoon may not have been the best time for a meeting that he finds stressful.

The challenge for the manager who wants to know self is to make a clear distinction between confidence and competence, to delegate to the person who is more competent in budgeting than he is and to hold such meetings at a time when his energy is likely to be high. Confidence is the knowing that one has limitless intelligence to learn anything. Competence is the actual learning of a particular area of knowledge or skill. It is very difficult to learn a subject if you doubt your ability to learn it. So many people complain that, for example, 'I'm useless at figures'. It is important that managers know and regularly affirm for themselves their immense potential to learn. Developing competence comes with study and practice.

The manager who knows self frequently reflects on all aspects of his life and will work to bring about change in behaviours that are problematic. He is a risk-taker, an adventurer and has a love of learning. He is ambitious, not only in his career, but in all aspects of living — physical, sexual, emotional, social, intellectual, behavioural, creative and spiritual. He is a major asset to any work organisation.

CHAPTER 3

MANAGERS WHO DO NOT KNOW THEMSELVES

MANAGEMENT IS NOT A GENDER ISSUE

The word 'manage' when hyphenated — man-age — is not the most accurate of terms to describe leadership behaviour. There is absolutely no guarantee that being a man or being a woman equals being effective at managing. After all, most men have rejected the feminine qualities that are so necessary for balanced and progressive management — empathy, compassion, ability to comfort, to show love, to be tender, to be kind, to be able to cry, to be able to stay with those who are upset, to nurture, to enable, to be reflective, and to be expressive and receptive to all the emotions. Men tend to be more comfortable with the 'masculine' qualities of hardness, firmness, drive, ambition, control, invention, order, thought, action, taking charge, being dynamic, creative and adventurous.

Certainly, masculine characteristics have contributed to much of what is good in the world, but because these qualities are not tempered by the feminine qualities, the tendency is for men to go to the extremes of masculine action and, sadly, much of what is wrong with the world can be attributed to this imbalance. Examples of the extremes of masculine qualities are aggression, violence, arrogance, dominance, over-control, possessiveness, competitiveness, pressurised life-style, rigidity, hostility, cynicism, sarcasm, denial, supremacy, superiority.

Of course, being a woman is no guarantee either that you will be effective as a manager. Women tend to be comfortable with the 'feminine' qualities of ability to nurture, to listen, to be tender, gentle, kind, compassionate, to be supportive, to be empathic, to be able to cope with upsetting feelings of another and to be expressive of most feelings. The problem is that when these qualities are not tempered and balanced by 'masculine' qualities, they operate at extreme levels and block effective leadership. The extremes of feminine qualities are passivity, over-caring to the point that it disables the receiver, helplessness, timidity, being over-wrought, hysteria, manipulativeness, obsessiveness, over-pleasing, dependence and a neglect of self.

One wonders, if those male managers who bully, harass and intimidate, who are viciously competitive, who are dismissive, arrogant and intolerant, possessed some of the feminine qualities, e.g. the ability to nurture, to enable, to be compassionate and tender, would it be possible for them to engage in such threat-ening behaviours? I don't believe it would. Similarly, if women managers who are passive, manipulative, perfectionist, non-expressive of their needs, who tolerate harassment and rudeness from workers or higher management possessed the masculine qualities of sureness, definitiveness, assertiveness, drive, ambition, the ability to take charge and set clear boundaries, would they persist with their passive behaviours that are threatening to themselves and, indeed, to the workers? I don't believe they would.

Effective management is both a head and heart phenomenon and an inward and outward movement. 'Masculinity' is essentially a head and outward movement. 'Femininity' is essentially a heart and inward movement. Effectiveness is determined by the possession of both sets of qualities. It behoves those men who are fearful of expressing their feminine side to seek the safety of overcoming such fear and come into the full breadth of human qualities. Equally, it behoves women who are fearful of expressing their masculine side to find the safety of overcoming such inhibition and bring forth the fullness of what it means to be human. All social systems — family, school, church, workplace, community and government — need to provide opportunities and support and encouragement for the maturing process of their members.

The process of becoming effective in managing is not simply a matter of men finding their feminine side and women their masculine side. The fact is that many men come into their management role not only with the absence of many essential feminine qualities, but also with the absence of certain important masculine characteristics. Furthermore, the strategies they have developed for masking their vulnerabilities pose a serious threat to the well-being of workers, the well-being of the organisation and, indeed, their own well-being. A resolution of underlying fears and vulner-abilities and a realisation of one's potential are part and parcel of becoming an effective manager. The same is true for women in management who enter their role with not only the absence of certain feminine qualities, but the absence of a range of masculine qualities. Like men, women hide their inner conflicts behind a whole range of masking behaviours that threaten their own, their employees' and the organisation's well-being.

The age of a manager, whether male or female, provides no grounds for optimism regarding the ability to manage effectively. Contrary to popular perception, age is no index of maturity; and neither for that matter are education or life experiences. Education and life experiences may have provided you with academic or street knowledge but, at the same time, you may have made no inroads into resolving the emotional issues that block you from being mature, real and authentic. Age does not mature us, but reflection and action do. Western society does not encourage and support us to ask and answer questions such as: 'Who am I?'; 'What am I doing here?'; 'What work fulfils my sense of self and provides service to the community?' Nonetheless, such questions deal with the essential issues that underline human maturity.

MANAGERS WHO DON'T KNOW SELF

No matter what you do, where you go, what relationships you enter into, you carry your emotional baggage with you, whether or not you like it, or whether or not you are conscious of it. No matter what level of responsibility you have or what your current work or social status is, how you see and feel about yourself will have a telling effect on how effective and efficient you are and how you view your current status within the work organisation. Your knowledge of and feelings about yourself not only determine how you relate to yourself, but also profoundly affect how you are with others and how you carry out your management responsibilities.

Your management style is not determined by the ethos of your organisation but by your own sense of self and of others, even though I do believe that organisations get the kind of manager they deserve. Obviously your levels of experience, knowledge and skill play a large part, but the cornerstone of effective leadership is the extent to which you know yourself.

What is meant by the term 'emotional baggage'? Emotional baggage is something we 'carry' from our early experiences. It is the sum of all the fears, insecurities and doubts that we have learned to have about ourselves and that we bring into our various roles in life. Our fears, insecurities and doubts manifest themselves in a variety of defensive ways, depending on our individual history and the unique ways we find to defend self against further hurt, humiliation, and a demeaning or lessening of our presence. Examples of such defences are aggression, manipulation, passivity, jealousy, competitiveness, a stressful lifestyle and dependence on others for approval.

The problem with defensive behaviours is that these in turn lessen the presence of others, leading to further defensive behaviour on their part. A whole defensive cycle of neglect now emerges. It is only when one person in the interaction proacts, rather than reacts, that there is a likelihood of progression towards mature relating and managing. Proaction arises from a mature possession of self and an acceptance and understanding of the true source of the defensive behaviour of the other. Regrettably, such mature responding is a rare phenomenon and much of the relating between managers and employees operates at a protective level.

How do we accumulate emotional baggage? From a very early age, we learn that many aspects of our dynamic self are not well received by important adults in our lives. Indeed, our manifestation of self is often greeted with defensive responses such as impatience, aggressive shouting, ridicule, scolding, demeaning words, shaming, violence, comparison, intolerance and shows of disappointment. In essence, we learn to repress or suppress those aspects of ourselves that have led to painful experiences. The aspects of self that are most commonly repressed or suppressed are: spontaneity, adventuresomeness, excitement, love of learning, love of work, the acceptance of failure and success as integral partners in the thrilling process of learning and working, expression of feelings, openness to receiving, high energy, intuitiveness, uniqueness and individuality.

It is truly remarkable how each of us, in spite of many attempts to make us the same, forges an individual way to be in the family and, later on, in the school and workplace. Each child within a family has a different parent, each student in a classroom has a different teacher, and each employee has a different manager. This is so because when two unique individuals interact, the interaction is unique. Managers who believe that the best policy is to treat all employees in the same way, will encounter major difficulties because the ultimate desire of each employee is to be seen, valued and appreciated for his/her unique self.

Of course, the manager who adopts the 'I treat all the employees the same' policy is out of touch with many aspects of his own individuality. One of the cleverest defences we learn when we are children is to conform, to 'not rock the boat', or 'not upset the applecart', and many managers bring that defensive ploy into their leadership roles. The follow-on is that they then expect workers to conform to their ways, and so the cycle of the suppression of individuality is perpetuated. The sad thing is that individuality is now manifested through defensiveness and not through creativity and productivity.

A distinction needs to be made between the defensive strategies of 'repression' and 'suppression'. Repression is the more serious defensive response because it occurs at a very early stage of life, usually during the first three years, and is done at a subconscious level. When the threat to revealing an aspect of self is terrifying, the infant or toddler hides that aspect of self in a way that does not remain in the consciousness. For example, to cry is a natural and powerful expression of hurt and of threat to the self, but when crying is responded to with extreme harshness, the infant learns not to cry. How very clever this is. I have treated many men who had repressed this aspect of self. They come with the complaint, 'I can't cry. No matter how sad or devastatingly shocking the situation is, I cannot cry.' They have no conscious memories of the harsh treatment that led to the repression of this powerful emotional expression. Gradually, through the safety of the therapeutic relationship, memories begin to surface and a readiness slowly emerges to express what they had dared not express for many years.

The manager who 'cannot cry' or 'hides his tears' will fail utterly in the face of an employee who cries and needs comforting concerning some aspect of the working relationship that is causing upset.

Suppression is a conscious 'bottling up' of a feeling or thought or a blocking of an action that, though needed, is too frightening to express. In many cases, while we may realise that we are pushing down a response, we may not consciously know why. But, because the defence of suppression is in our consciousness, the path to freeing ourselves of our fears is not as painful, complex or time-consuming as is the process of release from repression. Nonetheless, the suppression of any aspect of self is not easily undone. The rewards of release from defensive strategies of repression and suppression are to become real, spontaneous and free.

The weight and extent of our emotional baggage and the resultant levels of repression and suppression manifesting in our current stage of life are a reflection of the amount of hurt, humiliation and demeaning of aspects of our unique self experienced in childhood. These experiences were a product of the fact that the significant adults, siblings and peers we encountered in our young lives related to us from a defensive rather than an open and mature position. They did this, not out of a desire to hurt or block us, but because our free expressiveness was a threat to their blocked expressiveness. Managers can act only from their current level of maturity; the challenge of knowing self and freeing self of emotional baggage becomes an urgent responsibility when managers operate from a defensive position. Each one of us as adults, and not just managers, has a responsibility to know and understand ourselves so that we can better know and understand others and be more effective in the carrying out of our work and all other responsibilities.

THE SELF

What is meant by the 'self'? We talk about my-self, your-self, our-selves. Psychologists refer to an individual's self-esteem, self-image, self-concept, self-perception. Psychotherapists encourage self-affirmation, self-appraisal, self-observation, self-care, and speak of helping individuals to recover a sense of self and to rediscover the self of the other. Christ spoke about the love of self. Buddha said, 'Nobody is more deserving of love than yourself.' Socrates taught: 'Know thy self'. Ancient Indian texts advise that individuals need to be loved 'for the sake of the self', not for some particular life-role, such as being married, being a parent, working, or having high academic, career, political or religious status.

Valuing individuals on the basis of their roles in life or social or career position is a very serious issue because it denies our fundamental worth as human beings. For example, if I love my father for being my father, then should he choose to leave the family for some reason such as marital breakdown or deep personal vulnerability, does that mean I am going to act as if he no longer deserves my love? Fathering is an important social responsibility, but what makes the person who parents me lovable is his unique self. I may be emotionally devastated or hurt or disappointed or enraged when his fathering of me is no longer present in the way it was, but it is crucial that I do not confuse the parenting behaviours of the man who fathers me with his self, which is always deserving of love. Of course, withdrawal happens time and time again when someone no longer performs the role for which I valued them: 'You're no father of mine since you abandoned me and my mother'; 'I never want to see you again since you had an affair with that woman'; 'I could seriously hurt your chances of promotion if you don't toe the line.'

People in positions of management need to understand that the self is separate from anything the person does. The self refers to the unique presence of each person and is totally separate from any behaviour shown, be it excellent, good, mediocre, poor, bizarre, violent, passive, manipulative. When self and behaviour become enmeshed, all sorts of defensive behaviours emerge. For example, if a manager believes that it is success that makes his self worthy of recognition, a defensive addiction to success emerges and work now becomes a significant source of threat to the self. This manager will strive relentlessly to maintain a successful performance, at the cost of neglect of self, marriage, family, employees and colleagues.

The primary need of human beings is to be loved for self and to love others for their selves. Following on that primary longing are the needs for meaning to one's life, to learn to be productive and for attainments to be recognised and appreciated, but never confused with the self.

It is readily understood that if an employee makes a mistake and his manager publicly berates and humiliates him/her, this is likely to lead to a defensive response on the part of the employee. The defensive response may be an aggressive retort, a passive withdrawal or a passive-aggressive pulling back, with a determination 'to get back at the manager'. What is not so readily understood is that a label such as 'brilliant', applied to an employee who achieves the set targets, also reflects enmeshment of the employee's behaviour with himself and will also result in insecurity, with the employee now fearful of losing that status position. Certainly, the manager needs to praise work attainments and be specific in his use of praise words; for example: 'Thank you for the extra efforts made that led to achieving the targets set.' But praise of effort and behaviour is completely different to valuing the self of the person on the basis of effort or behaviour.

The issue is – and it is not a benign issue that managers can choose to ignore, either in relationship to themselves or their employees – you always affirm the self and you praise and encourage specific behaviours.

More and more I try to avoid labelling people according to their behaviour or career. For myself, I prefer to say 'I practise clinical psychology' rather than 'I'm a clinical psychologist.' Similarly, I make efforts to say 'I enjoy writing books and articles', rather than labelling myself as a writer. The self is beyond all behaviour; it precedes all behaviour and I believe survives when all behaviour ceases.

THE DEFENCES

Defences are subconscious or conscious strategies that arise when threats, real or perceived, to being oneself are present. The greater 'the threat', the greater the defence. It is important to understand that the threats experienced come from the defensive behaviour of others, who themselves are in a place of either real or perceived peril. Once others feel themselves to be under threat, they will not be able to respond openly to realness and authenticity on the part of the other person. A real threat is one that is directly experienced, such as somebody putting you down in front of others, being rude and abusive. A threat is perceived when it is not being directly experienced but you anticipate it arising. For example, if your experience of people in authority has been one of being controlled, criticised and demeaned, then your understandable tendency will be to perceive threats, whether there or not, from any person occupying a position of authority. It may take a long time without direct experience of a threat before you let your guard down with a person in authority and find the safety to be real.

Defences can be intrapersonal or interpersonal in nature. The strategy in an intrapersonal defence is to put yourself down or neglect self or suppress feelings before somebody else can do it. Furthermore, this type of defence prepares you for the shock of being rejected by another. It also makes it less likely that you will take the risk of being real and open with another. The ploy is to be your own worst enemy, thereby disarming the enemy without and to be passive so that others are put in the position of being active and having to take the risk of rejection that you have cleverly sidestepped.

The strategy in interpersonal defences is to control others before they can control you. The ploy is to be so intimidating or manipulative of others that they dare not ask things of you that you would perceive as threatening to your expression of self. For example, a manager may be continually cross, cynical and sarcastic in order to ensure that workers do not 'cross' him or contradict him or voice needs that he would be fearful of not being able to meet. Male managers who experience threat tend to be dominating in their style of leadership, thereby making it threatening for employees to question their decisions. At meetings of employees and managers, passivity among the employees is often the counter-defence to the aggression of the manager. Because both managers and employees are operating from a position of defence, little progress can be made at such meetings. As a result, the ethos of the workplace will be threatening, and effectiveness and efficiency greatly reduced.

Intrapersonal defences are an inward movement and inter-personal defences an outward movement. In both cases the intention is to stop hurt, but, paradoxically, the hurt you try to prevent for self may now be experienced by the other. Take the case of the manager who employs the defence of passivity – the most common intrapersonal defence. Others in his employ are likely to experience the hurt of his not being able to champion their rights and needs. In the case of the manager who employs the most common interpersonal defence – aggression – the hurt that others may experience is very evident.

Within each of the two main categories of defences, there exist several sub-categories, as is shown in the following examples.

Intrapersonal defences (inward and passive protective movement)

COGNITIVE

- Sees self as useless
- Wants always to be better than anyone else
- Dreads failure

EMOTIONAL

- Suppresses certain feelings, such as fear, anger
- Feels sorry for self
- Hates self

BEHAVIOURAL

- Does not respond to inner needs for nurturance, comfort and rest
- Pressure on self to get everything right

SEXUAL

- Addicted to self-stimulation
- Feels 'dirty' because of sexual feelings
- Suppresses sexual feelings

→

PHYSICAL

☐   Hates his/her physical appearance

☐   Pays no attention to physical needs

☐   Overeats or undereats

CREATIVE

☐   Believes he/she possesses no talents

☐   No valuing of own creative efforts

☐   Does not internalise positive feedback

On reading through these examples of intrapersonal defences it may not be apparent that they are protective in nature but remember that the purpose of each defence is to protect from some real or perceived threat to self. Some of the cognitive defences are more obvious in their protective function. For example, seeing yourself as 'useless' has the protective functions of eliminating any risk-taking and avoiding having any expectations of self. Of course, the exhibition of such apathy will also reduce other people's expectations of you.

The suppression of certain feelings, such as anger or fear, serves the protective purpose of removing the threat that is felt in acting outwards and asking for what you deserve in this world. It is a commonplace observation that women have suppressed their anger; there are good reasons for this as it is a strategy they have had to learn in order to reduce the possibilities of violence to or diminishment of their presence. On the other hand, men have tended to suppress their fears in order to protect themselves against being labelled 'weak' or 'namby-pamby' or 'mother's boy'.

The behaviour of not showing kindness to self can be a defence against the threat of ridicule and rejection from others which might come from attaching importance to self. For example, 'you're getting above yourself' or 'why do you think you should deserve kindness or attention?' are painful reminders to some individuals of how any assertion of one's unique presence can be harshly punished. The addiction to sexual self-stimulation may not readily be seen as defensive in nature. For individuals who have had little joy in life, compulsive masturbation can be a means of diluting the stark reality of not being celebrated and loved for self.

There are few individuals I know who possess a strong sense of their distinct physicality. Many of us cleverly have learned to hide any sense of our individual physical self as a defence against the threat that arises either through a passive type of parenting or one in which we were compared physically to others, or were never affirmed in our unique physical presence. The cleverness in repression or suppression of your unique physicality is that it serves to reduce the possibility of further annihilation of your physical presence.

All children have their own creative ways of doing things; if such creativity is not seen and valued, but, on the contrary, is ridiculed or scorned, children learn to hide their creativity from self and from others. The poignant issue is that the very creativity that could have added so much to the unique expression of self and contributed to the benefit of others and the world around becomes employed in the development of creative defences.

When a manager comes into his role of leadership with considerable intrapersonal defences, these will adversely affect his ability to function in this role. This is true too (even to a greater degree) of interpersonal defences.

Interpersonal defences

VERBAL

☐	highly critical
☐	sarcastic
☐	cynical

NON-VERBAL

- Rigid posture
- Aggressive tone of voice
- Poor eye contact

BEHAVIOURAL

- Pushing and shoving
- Rushing and racing
- Setting unrealistic targets

EMOTIONAL

- Ridiculing any display of upset
- Being continuously angry with others
- Being unable to cope with conflict

SOCIAL

- Avoiding staff outings
- Remaining alone in the canteen
- Mixing only with the 'in' people

PHYSICAL

- Missing meals
- Continuing to work when tired
- Ignoring stress signals

SEXUAL

- Frequent sexual innuendoes
- Sexually harassing staff members
- Using sexuality to manipulate others

The frequency and intensity of both intrapersonal and inter-personal defences are important barometers of the kind of ethos a manager creates in the workplace. Of equal importance is how long the defensive responses last at the time they occur and how long these threatening responses have endured over time – one year, two years, five, ten!

The interpersonal protectors are much more obviously a source of threat to the well-being of others. Common managerial defensive responses that threaten the presence and the identity of employees are: verbal harassment, impatience, intolerance, unre-alistic targets, cynicism, sarcasm, ridicule, a demanding tone of voice, lack of appreciation, lack of consultation, comparisons with other workers, unapproachability and unavailability. All these man-agerial protective behaviours create a circular defensive reaction on the part of employees and so a dark cycle of protectiveness is perpetrated.

LIVING FROM THE OUTSIDE IN

When you live life from the outside in, you allow yourself to be controlled by people and forces outside of yourself. The most common addiction of all is the addiction to what others say about you. It is easy to see how such an addiction weakens your position as a manager. Certainly, worrying about how others view you will make it difficult for you to be real and decisive around issues that require resolution. The depth, intensity and endurance of this defensive behaviour will determine the extent of how unreal you will be as a manager. If the defence is strong, employees may covertly complain that you are 'unreal' and that it is impossible to know where they stand with you.

Another defensive behaviour that often dogs the feet of managers, and puts them at the mercy of work performance, is the fear of failure. It is not fear of failure itself that managers dread but the defensive responses of others to a failure on their part. So many organisations have a covert, and sometimes quite overt, policy that failure is not tolerated. Such a policy seriously darkens the ethos of the workplace, and managers and other employees will develop all sorts of defences around this threat to their well-being. The more popular defence is avoidance, as expressed in the shape of such attitudes as: 'do as little as possible for the most money', 'do not show initiative', 'don't take on extra responsibilities', 'blame others when things go wrong', 'don't question' and 'take the maximum sick leave'.

The next most frequent defence against possible humiliation following failure is aggression. The purpose of the aggression, whether it be on the part of the manager or another employee, is to intimidate, so that no one would dare point to any shortcoming or failure. All of us have witnessed the situation where huge effort is put into covering up what has gone wrong. In John Cleese's famous phrase, the push is 'don't mention the war', because if you do 'all hell will break loose'.

Yet another defensive behaviour displayed by managers and others is the addiction to success. Managers who protectively believe that success makes them important are doomed to a very difficult work life and will also doom employees to a difficult work life. It is a sad reality that there are very few managers who see work as it rightly deserves to be seen, that is as an adventure, a love affair, an excitement, an experiment, a wonderful challenge that in no way poses a threat to the self. What counts in managing is not success, but progress towards enhancing relationship, realising both the manager's own and the employees' potential and the enjoyment of work attainment.

IT'S THE INTENTION THAT COUNTS

While it is important that individual managers and the work organisation try to understand protective responses by attempting to detect the causes of these, it is equally important to understand the intention of defensive behaviours. The intention of a defensive behaviour is not to hurt or threaten another, even though that is often what happens. No, the intention is to guard against whatever source of threat is being perceived by the person who engages in the defensive practices. The threats can be the possibility of failure, of criticism, of being 'shown up', of not knowing something, of being humiliated, of being laughed at, of not reaching targets, of not being good enough. Only the individual manager, either subconsciously or consciously, knows what is causing the threat, but it is crucial for others to appreciate that the difficult behaviour being displayed by the manager is one hundred per cent about his hidden vulnerabilities.

There is no suggestion here that defensive behaviour should be excused on the basis that 'he didn't mean it'. What is being emphasised is that, when confrontation comes from an appreciation of the causes and an understanding of the intention of defensiveness, then it is far more likely to be effective in resolving the conflict. Judgement, lack of understanding and intolerance also reflect defensiveness and serve only to exacerbate the manager's defensive behaviour; clearly no mature resolution is now possible.

'THE GOOD, THE BAD, THE UGLY'

Even though I have encountered many ugly scenes in the managerial world, I believe it is a mistake to categorise managers as 'good', 'bad', or 'ugly'. Managers are not their behaviour, whether that behaviour is mature or defensive. Indeed, those managers who are labelled 'good' are often caught in the defensive trap of having to prove themselves all the time and they can put immense pressure on themselves and on workers to maintain their 'good' label. Creating such pressure and being work-addicted do not make for good management, either in the short or long term. Organisations may feel that they are fortunate to have such a 'good' manager, and in the short term this manager may be highly productive — but at a cost to self, to others and, eventually, to the organisation. In the long term this manager will begin to struggle, may experience burnout, become depressed, suffer psychosomatic illnesses and begin to rely on drugs or alcohol to get him through the day. Absenteeism and sickness are likely to ensue and the cost to the company can now be high.

The 'goodness' in management lies in mature relating, realistic expectations and attention to the full spectrum of human needs, not just to work needs.

In the same way that there are no 'good' managers, neither are there 'bad' or 'ugly' managers. To confuse the person of the manager with his managerial style, no matter how appalling, is a defensive and judgemental response on the part of others and serves only to exacerbate a difficult situation. Certainly the 'bad' or 'ugly' practices need to be confronted, preferably by the manager himself and, in the absence of managerial self-action, expediently by the organisation. The organisation needs to have structures that ensure that no member of the organisation is at risk from another, whether that be employee from manager or *vice versa*. When there are no back-up structures to deal with neglect, the fall-out in terms of human misery in the workplace is likely to be considerable.

SEEING ONLY WHAT YOU ARE READY TO SEE

When managers or employees engage in defensive reactions, they mostly do so quite subconsciously and can be shocked when confronted about their threatening behaviours. A common response is 'I didn't realise I was causing such pain' or 'I had no idea I was diminishing of the employee.' The word 'realise' is accurate; when you 'realise' something you are getting ready to come to terms with the *reality* of your defensive responses and to begin to access what lies hidden behind those protective behaviours. Up to the point of realisation, the focus is on hiding aspects of self that you feel you dare not show. Paradoxically, the act of confrontation creates an opportunity for the manager to reflect on and discover what lies behind his defensive actions.

But surely, you ask, a manager who is aggressive, cynical and sarcastic sees the upset he is causing to others? Actually he does not; in his defensiveness, he will perceive the other person's upset as being 'a weakness' and will not attribute the upset to his defensive actions. This clever defensive strategy is known as *rationalisation*; the strategy allows you to find what appears to be a rational explanation for the other's upset and enables you to skirt the need to reflect on your own behaviour. The manager who engages in rationalisation is in no way ready to begin to examine his threatening behaviour; a safe emotional environment needs to be created before such a transformation will be possible. Typical rationalisations are: 'he drove me to it', 'their behaviour was outrageous'; 'they're impossible to work with'; 'I seem to have been lumbered with a ship of fools'; 'it's the only way to get any results around here.'

Defences will remain unrecognised or rationalised or projected on to others until the manager is ready to reflect on his actions. Even when solidly, respectfully and clearly confronted, a manager with a strong set of defences may see the organisation as 'going soft' or 'the powers-that-be pandering to employees who can't take a bit of stick' or 'the organisation taking up those cracked feminist notions'. When a manager is deeply stuck in his defences, the organisation may need to resort to a temporary suspension of duties and the provision of an opportunity for the manager to consult professional therapeutic help. No return to his management position can be allowed until the manager has recovered some sense of self, realises his defensive ways and is now willing to adopt more mature and real ways of leadership.

CHAPTER 4

MANAGERS WHO KNOW THEIR EMPLOYEES

THE QUEST OF KNOWING EMPLOYEES

Without jeopardising the boundaries that are needed around their own responsibilities, managers who want to know their staff seek knowledge of individual employees from appropriate sources. They want to know only about those areas of an employee's life that are relevant to the managerial role, to the organisation's expectations of the employee and to the employee's personal well-being and career progress. They ensure that any information gained is kept confidential. They want the employee to know that they are considerate of his/her person and marital and family relationships and are available and approachable to provide support in any of these key areas. They are aware that the quest of knowing staff members needs to spring from a place of genuine concern; it is not a 'new age' exercise read in some book or heard at some course in management skills. In any case, managers know that any hint of manipulation on their part will be picked up intuitively by employees, who will then close the door to their knowing more about them.

Before ever encountering an individual employee, managers know certain essential facts about the person. They know that he/she is unique, an individual with limitless potential and that he/she brings special giftedness to the workplace. Managers are also aware that he/she will perceive them from an individual perspective and that they need to be sensitive to the nuances of this unique relationship. They know that the employee brings a history different to all others to the workplace and that his/her sense of self can play an important part in determining the quality of the work ethos. In their interactions with the employee, they will seek to affirm all these 'givens' about him/her and thereby create the safety for that person to express those essential aspects of self.

From the selection interview and curriculum vitae, managers can gain some knowledge of the worker's present life circumstances, marital and family status, educational history, work experiences, work achievements, ambitions, hobbies and interests. However, it will be in their everyday interactions with the worker that they can verify what they have read, heard and observed during the selection process. The old saying 'if you want to know me, then come live with me' can be adapted to the work situation: 'if you want to know your employee then you need to work alongside him/her'.

The most effective way to get to know another person is through systematic observation. Managers need to be trained in observation techniques, so that they can evaluate not only the worker's knowledge, skills, application and commitment to work responsibilities, but also the nature of that person's relating to self, co-workers, management and clients of the organisation. It is by his/her actions that managers can truly get to know their employee's ways of being in, and, to some degree outside, the workplace. Of course workers can present themselves one way in the workplace and be quite the opposite in their homes; it is never wise to assume that behaviours, 'good', 'bad' or 'indifferent', in one situation generalise to other situations.

Open days for staff and their families can provide a further opportunity for getting to know workers and, where relevant, their partners and children. The manager needs to guard against being intrusive and, after welcoming the family members, take his cue from how they respond to his friendliness and make sure to not outstay his welcome.

The manager who is 'person friendly' wants to know the individual staff member's ambitions, creativity, particular giftedness and aspirations. Such knowledge provides the opportunities for the manager and the work organisation to enable the worker's potential. Career progress within the organisation needs to be based on the manager's unbiased knowledge of the employee across the dimensions of work attainments, personal care, relationships and leadership qualities.

EMPLOYEES MANAGERS *CAN'T STAND*

Where managers have a reaction to the presence or the behaviour of an individual employee, they need to recognise this as their opportunity to deepen their own knowledge of themselves and, where necessary, express their needs to this employee. All managers have had the experience of 'not being able to stand the sight of' some particular employee or having little or no tolerance for certain behaviours exhibited by a particular staff member. The reactions that arise within managers are windows into hidden parts of self that the presence or the behaviour of this worker are triggering. The worker who presents a nervous, jittery, timid and unsure presence can 'get on the nerves' of managers who like to perceive themselves as 'doers'. It may be the case that these managers have difficulty 'taking a back seat', that they do not know that listening is more important that speaking or doing. They may also have difficulty in admitting that they themselves are unsure or fearful. If managers are able to express these particular aspects of self, they will be more accepting of the unsure presence that the employee exhibits. Their reactions to the employee are opportunities for them to discover and reflect on those parts of self they have become fearful of manifesting.

A worker who presents an 'overbearing' and 'know it all' presence may trigger defences in managers who tend to be indecisive and look for considerable reassurance before making a decision. It is not that managers need to become 'overbearing' but they do need to aim for the golden mean between the two defensive extremes — overbearing, on the one hand, and fear of taking risk on the other hand. It is a well-known fact that opposites tend to attract and, subsequently, react to each other. In every defensive behaviour lies the possibility of open and mature responding. For instance, aggression is a common defence whereby an individual uses verbal or physical force to have a need met. Being assertive and determined are important aspects of standing on one's own two feet and are far removed from aggressive responses. The essential difference is that aggression arises from insecurity about the ability to be responsible for self — and the aggressive responses are designed 'to make' the other person responsible for you, while assertiveness arises from the certainty of being able to hold one's own and the assertive responses are designed to ensure that you do just that. Mature and open behaviours are always respectful of self and of others; defensive responses do not demonstrate such respect.

In situations where managers find themselves reacting to a behaviour that is opposite to their own typical behavioural repertoire, they should take the opportunity to explore this question: 'what are the aspects of this employee's ways of acting that I cannot stand and that I dare not show, and how can I achieve the golden mean between my defensive and his defensive stance?' When managers find themselves reacting defensively to the presence of an employee, they need to ask themselves the question: 'what is it in me that is preventing me from seeing the unique worth and presence of this employee?'

Sometimes it is a particular behaviour rather than the employee's presence that grates on managers; for example, being obsequious, being loud, non-listening, always late, engaging in smart-aleck behaviour. Clearly, such behaviours can block particular needs of managers and can lead to conflict. In the examples given, the blocked needs of managers may be wanting a worker to show respect for himself/herself, to talk in a mature and calm way, to listen, to be on time and not to engage in hostile humour. These are all legitimate needs but if managers simply react against the employee, then they are not doing too well in expressing and taking responsibility for their own needs. Managers who want to know themselves and know their employees will avail of this opportunity to assert their own particular blocked needs. They will also seek to understand the defensive behaviours of workers and provide opportunities for them to free themselves in the particular behaviours that they are fearful of showing in an open, straightforward way.

EMPLOYEES WHO *RESIST BEING KNOWN*

There are some employees who will resist the good intentions and actions of managers who seek to know them. The sources of this resistance to being known lie within the employee and, more than likely, lie at a subconscious level. The resistance may manifest itself in several ways: avoiding eye contact and verbal contact, monosyllabic answers to enquiries, showing hostility to benign actions, 'laughing off' the manager's efforts to know them and being downright rude. It is important that managers do not personalise these difficult responses, that they do not attack back, and that when their presence is lessened by the employee's behaviour they express their need for a respectful response.

It is sometimes the case that the employee who blocks the good efforts of a manager is hiding some covert defences that may jeopardise his/her job situation – for example, alcohol addiction, drug addiction, pilfering, past misdemeanours in previous workplaces, false claims in curriculum vitae. Where managers are mature, it is only a matter of time before they begin to spot the signs of such defences. It is also not uncommon for employees to fear being known because they feel nobody could like them or that people might perceive them as 'slow' or 'not too bright' or because they are ashamed of a poor family background or poor education.

Should there be persistent resistance, it would not be wise for the manager to pursue his quest of knowing the worker. What the manager can be sure of is that employees who defend self from being known by another do not know themselves and considerable safety at all levels (physical, sexual, emotional, intellectual, social, creative and behavioural) is needed if there is to be any chance of their allowing themselves to be known. More than likely, in addition to the ongoing efforts of the manager, the organisation may need to provide the opportunity for psychotherapy. Should these attempts not bear fruit, then the manager and the organisation may consider the difficult decision of terminating the employee's employment.

OBSERVATION: THE KEY TO KNOWING EMPLOYEES

There is no more reliable way of knowing another person than through observation. Managers and employees spend as many, if not more, hours in each other's company than do a couple, or a working parent with children. All this time allows for systematic observation along the lines of the following:

☐ what actions of the employee enhance/block the relationship between the manager and the employee?

- what actions of the employee enhance/block the relationship between the organisation and the employee?
- what actions of the employee enhance/block work effectiveness?
- what actions of the employee enhance/block staff morale?

The actions observed may occur in or across all the main categories of human behaviour already spoken about — physical, sexual, emotional, intellectual, behavioural, social, financial and creative. Astute managers not only observe with their eyes but also listen attentively with their ears, so they begin to know how the employee responds in different situations when they are around and not around. The following list indicates some possible observations:

- contact with colleagues
- body language
- time-keeping
- level of initiative
- motivation
- ambition
- level of ease in asking for information or help when needed
- response to new challenge
- work commitment
- work rate
- listening skills
- presence or absence of clock-watching
- relationships, family, children
- attendance at staff outings
- participation at staff meetings
- energy level
- physical and psycho-social well-being
- interactions with colleagues (superior, inferior, equal, gossips, complains, is aggressive, is passive)
- sense of humour
- educational history
- educational interests
- religion, spirituality
- problem-solving skills
- responses to conflict
- responses to positive feedback
- responses to requests for change

In observing individual staff members, managers are not only keen to get to know each person more fully, they are also watchful of how individual employees interact. Group presence is greatly influenced by what each staff member brings to the group in terms of his/her presence or behaviour. Group presence or staff morale is the collective of what level of maturity each employee, including the manager, brings to the workplace. Managers are alert to the fact that the emotional baggage of one or more employee can adversely affect staff morale and they see it as their responsibility to ensure that the defensive behaviours of the few do not jeopardise the well-being of any individual employee or the group morale.

In all their interactions with staff members, managers are on first-name terms and request that they be addressed by their first name. They are particularly watchful of the language they use because language is deeply reflective of the attitudes we hold. They are quick to spot in themselves (and staff members) language that is dogmatic, domineering, rigid, inflexible, patronising, superior, passive, timid, aggressive or offensive and are not slow to apologise for such 'slips of the tongue'.

FEEDBACK AS A POWERFUL WAY TO GET TO KNOW EMPLOYEES

Managers who want to know their workers can employ feedback on work attainments as an opportunity to enhance relationship, to increase employees' skills, to raise motivation and to discover the work needs of the employees. Many employees hate what has become known as 'performance appraisal'. The use of the word 'performance' is unfortunate because it puts the emphasis on a successful outcome, and not on progress or attainment. There are always ways to improve on work attainments but the nature of this enquiry is critical. Feedback on attainments rather than performance needs to be a joint venture, whereby the manager invites the employee to evaluate his/her attainments and they both look at possibilities for further progress. This is not being 'soft'; it is better that the employee evaluates self, rather than that the manager makes a judgement on what he considers to be the employee's value to the organisation. There is no suggestion here that the manager ignores poor work attainment, but movement is much more likely when the individual worker makes that assessment. In any case, if the manager or the organisation has specific needs of the employee, these need to be communicated to him/her in a way that reflects ownership of those needs and does not place blame on the employee. The manager's needs and the employee's attainments are two separate issues and their enmeshment with each other can lead to 'performance appraisal' being a dreaded experience.

Feedback, of its very nature, needs to be an act of nurturance.

CHAPTER 5

MANAGERS WHO DO NOT KNOW THEIR EMPLOYEES

KNOWLEDGE IS POWER

It is the wise manager who realises that knowledge is power: knowledge of self and knowledge of others. The manager who does not know himself is unlikely to know his employees in any meaningful way. Knowing workers is about affirming the unique and sacred presence of each employee, acknowledging how that uniqueness manifests itself in what employees think, say, do, dream and feel, appreciating employees' work efforts and creating opportunities for employees to realise their potential and unique giftedness. Certainly, those managers who defensively try to 'placate' employees or those who 'align' themselves with employees will tend to know aspects of the staff's lives that they can manipulate for their own defensive ends. However, they are not interested in knowing their employees for themselves, and the employee will see that and will close the door to any real openness. Indeed, these employees will tend to reveal only those aspects of their lives that 'fit in' with the defensive needs of their manager. There will also be those employees who will rebel and close down completely.

You may wonder why a manager needs to know his staff; is not the more important thing that he knows self? There is no doubt that the knowing of self is paramount to being an effective manager, but knowledge of those who work with you is also of crucial importance. The prime need of every human being is to love and be loved and while the word 'love' is taboo in many workplaces, the manager and the organisation that, wittingly or unwittingly, choose to ignore that key human need do so at their own peril. The manager who ridicules the notion of valuing employees for themselves and of being valued in turn for himself by the employee cannot be effective in what he does. Many employees complain about 'anonymity' in the workplace or 'lack of respect'; such complaints arise from managers who do not know their employees and organisations that do not promote affirmation of the unique presence of each person in the organisation.

Knowing employees is also basic to staff motivation. The manager's task of motivating employees rests on how much a manager knows self and knows employees, how much he loves his work and how he can inspire employees to love their work. Kahlil Gibran says that 'work is love made visible', but this is not a common phenomenon in the workplace. Nonetheless, one of the primary management tasks is to inspire in employees an eagerness to work. Employees tend to take their cues from managers and it is the manager who manifests adventuresomeness, challenge and love around work who is likely to inspire a similar motivation in his staff.

Of course, there are managers who abuse the knowledge they possess about employees by treating it as a mechanism to bully, control, embarrass or intimidate. Such a misuse of knowledge will always be counterproductive, because those who are victims of such behaviour will find passive, passive-aggressive or aggressive ways of defending themselves.

There are several areas of knowledge that managers need to pursue in regard to those with whom they work. There is no suggestion here that managers be intrusive or invasive; such behaviours are defensive in nature and will not serve any progressive purpose. The idea is that managers show interest in the unique presence of each employee and in his/her intrapersonal, interpersonal and work life. Such interest needs to spring from a genuine desire to know the person, having regard to the extent that that person is willing to reveal himself/herself. This process is not a one-way street; managers themselves need to be open to employees knowing them. Any hint that this process is a one-way street will quickly block its development.

The particular areas of knowledge that a manager could focus on in the process of getting to know his employees include the following:

- Physical — health, fitness, energy, dress
- Emotional — whether the employee expresses, suppresses, dilutes or is dismissive of his/her emotions
- Intellectual — whether interested in ideas, whether reflective, whether displays defences of superiority, inferiority
- Social — whether outgoing, whether quiet or vocal at meetings, whether doesn't mix, whether absent from work outings
- Educational — record to date, relevance of education to career, ambitions, attitude to learning
- Behavioural — whether arrogant, whether confident or timid, whether risk-taker, whether adventurous
- Creative — whether inventive, full of ideas, whether divergent or convergent
- Spiritual — beliefs, whether tolerant of difference, whether inspirational

The manager who lacks confidence may fear that inquiry into his employees' lives will show up his own deficiencies in his own and in others' eyes. Rather than genuinely seeking out information about the lives of his staff, the defensive manager will tend to observe only those behaviours and qualities that he can employ to 'knock' workers. 'Putting an employee down' has the subconscious purpose of trying to level a playing field that is experienced as uneven because of hidden vulnerability. This defence also has the purpose of attempting to ensure that the employee will not 'get ahead' of the manager. The examples below illustrate how the manager who is insecure will tend to notice physical, emotional, intellectual, educational, social, behavioural, creative and spiritual aspects of employees that he can employ for defensive purposes in times of threat and use derogatory terms to describe what he observes.

- Physical – labels such as 'ugly', 'tubby', 'pull through for a rifle', 'fat slob', 'sex bomb'
- Emotional – 'weak', 'goes all sloppy on you', 'cries at the drop of a hat', 'explosive', 'time-bomb'
- Intellectual – 'thick', 'stupid', 'know all', 'up in the clouds'
- Educational – 'should we call you doctor?', 'college graduate of sweet fuck all'
- Social – 'little Miss Perfect', 'wallflower', 'ass-licker'
- Behavioural – 'terrier', 'work horse', 'goes at a snail's pace', 'ball-hopper'
- Creative – 'Michelangelo', 'the Professor'
- Spiritual – 'Holy Mary'

It is not too difficult to imagine that when a manager interacts with staff members in these 'unknowing' and defensive ways, the consequences in terms of staff loyalty, motivation and productivity are disastrous.

TYPICAL BEHAVIOURS OF MANAGERS WHO DO NOT KNOW THEIR EMPLOYEES

Managers who are fearful of or do not consider the importance of getting to know their employees can manifest several of the following defensive behaviours:

- Being dismissive
- Being arrogant
- Being highly critical
- Being superior
- Being unavailable
- Being unapproachable
- Having no time for 'small talk'
- Engaging in interactions 'on the run'
- Not listening
- Having the attitude that only productivity matters
- Talking *at* workers
- Hiding away in office
- Being sarcastic
- Being cynical
- Engaging in nepotism
- Not knowing or calling workers by their first names
- Not being person friendly
- Not being family friendly
- Not being relationship friendly

Managers who exhibit these kinds of behaviours do so because they are very frightened of knowing employees and, as a consequence, do all in their power to block such a desirable process. The behaviour of 'non-listening' is one of the most powerful means of eliminating the development of any meaningful relationship between the defensive manager and his staff. Next to observation, listening is the most powerful way of getting to know employees. Its absence reveals the lack of the kind of inner listening by the manager that would enable him to get in touch with his own hidden vulnerability and that would open the way to freeing himself from its dark power. The manager who does not listen to self will find it safer to keep staff at bay, so that he will not have to face the formidable task of challenging his fears.

There are those managers who 'talk on the run', who are 'too busy to talk right now' — or who 'hide away in their offices' for fear of being challenged. All these managers not only miss the opportunities to get to know their staff, but miss out on employees knowing them.

The defence of putting productivity before people is quite a common one among managers in all types of organisations. Managers who subscribe to this attitude put major emphasis on 'deadlines', 'targets', 'competitiveness', no matter what the costs (physical, emotional, social) to employees' lives. There was a time when workplaces had what were known as 'personnel' departments, but the last two decades have seen the ugly rise of 'human resources' departments. The very title reflects the attitude to employees which has emerged and its deleterious effects are slowly but surely coming home to roost. Many organisations are now being sued for allowing bullying and harassment in the workplace and for reinforcing stressful working conditions. Employees cannot be equated with a resource you dig out of the ground and use as a means to the end of productivity. It must be recognised that each staff member brings giftedness, skills and a unique presence to the workplace.

Of course staff members, like managers, bring their emotional baggage, their 'not knowing' of themselves to the workplace, but it is the wise manager who sees these defences as opportunities to help workers to recover a sense of their true self and to maximise their unique potential and giftedness. The manager who feels threatened will 'rubbish' such sentiments and it is a dark organisation that fails to recognise this manager's oppressive presence and his effect on employees.

A more fitting and mature title for human resource departments that have the task of selecting, overseeing and resolving conflicts is 'Human Relationship Management'. The letters HR can be retained. However, I do not encourage the abbreviation of 'human relations' to HR since it represents a lessening of the importance of relationships in the workplace. Indeed, all management is about the enhancement of relationships.

RESPONSES OF EMPLOYEES TO MANAGERS WHO DO NOT KNOW THEM

Knowing employees, as has been defined here, is quite a tall order, and a threatening one to the manager who doubts self. When the manager does not know the workers and, instead, operates in ways that ridicule their unique ways of being, that ignore or are defensively critical of work efforts, that show no interest in maximising potential, employees need to respond powerfully to counteract this disinterest. The defensive counter-response is to cleverly find ways of 'putting down' the manager or of avoiding contact with him. The most common defence here is to gossip and create a clique that becomes a threat to the manager, who is unlikely 'to take on' the defensive power of this informally constituted group of employees.

Frequently, what the manager under siege does is to create his own cohort of loyal workers whom he grooms for membership of this 'inner' group through 'false' praise. It might seem that members of the inner sanctum have an advantage over the 'outer' group, but in reality the 'inner' members are far more under threat than the 'outsiders'. 'Insiders' dare not have an opinion of their own, dare not contradict and must demonstrate total loyalty to the immature leadership. Any slip from grace in this controlling situation can result in harsh expulsion from their seemingly privileged position. The strategy that can effectively pass among employees is to 'stay out of the way of this manager', 'don't trust him' and 'don't expect anything good'.

Counter-defences tend to be circular in their development. For example, an employee who is demeaned in some physical way by his manager will pick some physical 'flaw' in the manager to put down; if the manager labels that person as 'shorty', the employee's response may be to also label the manager's physical presence in a negative way — 'bull-head'; 'snake-eyes'; 'ugly bastard'. Similarly, in the emotional dimension, managers who are afraid to know their employees may in turn be labelled as 'gross', 'macho', 'emotionally thick', or 'heartless'. Intellectually, they may be referred to as 'zombies', 'illiterate', 'stupid', 'ignorant' and, educationally, as 'first grade', 'too thick to understand', 'dinosaur'. Socially, they will be avoided at all costs. Behaviourally, they will be seen as 'manipulative', 'limited' or 'unscrupulous opportunists' with no creative potential. Spiritually, they will be seen as 'dead'.

HOW MANAGERS WHO DO NOT KNOW THEMSELVES VIEW WORK

Managers who do not know themselves are likely to have attitudes towards work that not only significantly affect their management style, but also colour staff members' attitudes to work. Individuals work for all sorts of reasons, but managers who do not know themselves work for mainly defensive reasons.

- □ To prove themselves
- □ To be successful

- ☐ To overpower
- ☐ To impress others
- ☐ To fill an inner emptiness
- ☐ To create emotional distance
- ☐ To suppress a painful memory

These defensive reasons for working are an extension of defences that were present before they ever entered the workplace, and that is why it is difficult to distinguish between 'personal' and 'occupational' stressors. The latter are a function of the nature of work. For example, it appears that teaching is the most at-risk social profession and is more stressful than police work, medicine, dentistry, social work, or work as a prison warden. However, the difference in stress levels may have more to do with the particular individuals who are attracted to the profession than the profession itself. It is my belief that the level of personal maturity is the most significant barometer of level of work stress.

When managers work for any of the reasons outlined above, inevitably they will put pressure on workers to help them fulfil their defensive ambitions. Their concern is to protect themselves from failure and consequent hurt and humiliation; they are not in a place to be vigilant around the psycho-social well-being of their staff.

There is an inner emptiness in managers and employees who do not know themselves, a void that cries out to be filled with an acceptance and a knowing and loving of self. Experience has taught these individuals that taking time for self is perilous and so they have cleverly found a substitute way of filling the void — work. But a substitute can never be as effective as the real thing and the attempt to fill the void of distance from self with work never totally eases the ache. Similarly, managers who use work as 'a distance regulator' are fearful of real intimacy, because of their own lack of intimacy with self as a result of their earlier abandonment experiences. Long hours at work, bringing work home, setting up an office or study at home to which regular retreat is made; these are all clever ways of keeping intimacy at bay. The underlying defensive belief of these managers is that 'nobody could ever love me for myself', and so it is best to keep others — mother, father, wife, children — at arm's length.

CHAPTER 6

MANAGING FROM THE INSIDE OUT

MANAGING SELF

The manager who leads from the inside out knows well that his essential tasks are the enhancement of relationships with employees, the enablement of employees and a commitment to the realistic aspirations of the work organisation. Enhancing relationship involves ensuring that all interactions are of a nature that dignify the presence of the individual employees, ensuring that the work they do is worthy of their dignity and that their place of work is valuing of their presence. Enabling employees involves believing in the potential of each individual employee, practising the art of encouragement and effective appraisal of attainments and providing opportunities for employees to explore their giftedness and vast potential.

The manager who wants to lead from the inside out is fully aware that his ability to put that aspiration into practice is dependent on the extent to which he manages self; it is dependent on his sense of his own dignity and worthiness, on his possession of a strong belief in self and on his willingness to continue to explore his own giftedness and potential. Powerful leadership can come only from inner power. Possession of self lies on a continuum; a manager who may be in touch with some aspects of self may be totally blind to or fearful of exhibiting other aspects of self. In those aspects of self known to the manager it is likely that he will show effectiveness, but the absence of other qualities may shadow this effectiveness. For example, a manager may be in touch with and confident in his expression of his intellectual potential, but when this expression is not tempered by certain heart qualities he will be perceived as lacking warmth, emphathy and compassion.

True maturity lies in the possession of all the critical human qualities that contribute to emotional, social, intellectual, creative and spiritual well-being. While true maturing may not always be within our reach, it is wise for managers to seek the realisation of the full breadth of human qualities, particularly those that pertain to the relationship with self and to the relationship with others.

It is from the solid ground of knowing self that the manager can connect in meaningful, relevant, respectful and effective ways with others. All organisations need to have strong co-operation and support between managers and employees, managers and higher management and workers and workers. Such cooperation is more likely to emerge when the leadership is of a nature that prioritises relationships and guards against the anonymity of individual employees.

The manager who knows self will make it his business to know the workers and ensure that they know him. He knows his main managing task is to create a positive work ethos where each employee has a strong sense of visibility, where respectful relationships exist across the board, where job satisfaction is high and there is fair pay, where there is consideration for life-balance, where there are opportunities for career and educational progression and where there are back-up systems to deal with any neglect of employees. The manager is well aware that staff morale is the life-blood of the organisation and that open, congruent, authentic, direct and clear communication is the heart that pumps that life-blood.

Encouragement of group decision-making, availability, approach-ability, regular affirmation of the presence of individual staff members, and recognition, encouragement and praise of specific work efforts are all central to managing from the inside out. Congruence is only possible when the manager can relate in mature ways to self and from that inner relationship relate in similar ways to employees. Affirmation of the unique person of each employee and support and praise of work attainments ring true only when these behaviours emerge from the manager's own solid affirmation of self and realistic appraisal of his own work attainments.

QUALITIES OF MANAGERS WHO MANAGE FROM THE INSIDE OUT

There are multiple qualities that typify managers who lead from the inside out. There is no suggestion that a manager has to possess the full breadth of qualities listed below, but any significant falling short is best taken as an invitation to reflect more deeply on the style of management being practised. The excitement of this reflection is that new challenges will be thrown up to be hotly pursued.

A balance between the heart and head qualities is what is required.

Qualities of the manager who leads from the inside out

HEAD QUALITIES	HEART QUALITIES	HEAD/HEART QUALITIES
☐ is energetic	☐ is emotionally expressive	☐ knows self
☐ is sure		☐ inspires
☐ is responsible	☐ is emotionally receptive	☐ has a balanced lifestyle
☐ is confident		
☐ has clear vision of how the workplace needs to be	☐ actively listens	☐ is dynamic
	☐ is trustworthy	☐ effectively resolves conflicts/ problems
	☐ nurtures	
	☐ is considerate of the person, marriage, family	
☐ is assertive		☐ is independent
☐ enables workers		☐ is an adventurer
☐ is definite	☐ is insightful	☐ is open to feed-back, new ideas
☐ learns from mistakes	☐ is kind	
	☐ loves work	☐ is creative
☐ is firm on accountability	☐ is considerate	☐ is innovative
	☐ is caring	☐ is effective
☐ has capacity to empower	☐ is respectful	☐ is realistic
	☐ is affirming	☐ is appreciative
☐ consults with others	☐ is trustworthy	☐ acknowledges all contributions
	☐ is fearless	
☐ is flexible	☐ is loyal	☐ apologises when wrong
☐ fosters group decision-making	☐ is empathic	
	☐ is compassionate	☐ is approachable
☐ is persistent	☐ is encouraging	☐ is available
☐ is consistent	☐ is supportive	☐ has vision
☐ challenges	☐ seeks support	☐ is reflective
☐ confronts when necessary	☐ is spontaneous	☐ is humorous

→

HEAD QUALITIES (CONT.)

- believes in employees
- is determined
- practises direct and clear communication
- is a keen observer of behaviour
- is just and fair
- takes risks
- is committed
- knows the 'buck stops' with him
- sets clear boundaries
- is competent
- is efficient
- appreciates difference
- is insightful

HEART QUALITIES (CONT.)

- is exuberant
- is sensitive to others
- is in touch with own inner issues
- has ability to comfort those in distress

HEAD/HEART QUALITIES (CONT.)

- is optimistic
- knows about employees' lives
- is congruent
- recognises the individuality of each employee
- shows under-standing
- makes requests (not orders)
- is authentic

As already indicated, it has been the case that the 'head' qualities have tended to be found more in male managers and the heart qualities in female managers. This, of course, is not a genetic phenomenon, but a polarisation in the socialisation process, which is showing more and more signs of changing. Every human being, male and female, has the potential to develop the full breadth of human qualities and it is expedient that any persons in a leadership role set about the challenge of becoming more fully human.

ENHANCING WORKPLACE RELATIONSHIPS

The quality of workplace relationships is the main determinant of workplace effectiveness and, accordingly, the primary management task is to enhance relationships. While a manager cannot do much about the emotional baggage employees bring to the workplace, he can do a considerable amount about the interpersonal relationships that are there. It is the task of the selection process to ensure that those who are employed are not highly vulnerable but, no matter how good a selection process is, some level of vulnerability is brought by every employee, including managers, into the workplace. When the vulnerability is of a moderate nature, mature and empowering relationships formed in the workplace can have the positive effect of increasing the individual employee's feelings of security and confidence.

Traditionally, managers have not placed emphasis on relationships; this has been a defensive blindness that has led to considerable neglect of the welfare of employees. It does not take any more time to enhance relationships than it does to lessen a person's presence. Double standards do not work. Because members of work organisations tend to take their cues from those who hold the power, the manager needs to be vigilant that his ways of relating to staff members model how he wants them to relate to each other and to him. Commonsense tells us that employees who feel treated as individuals, who are respected and believed in, are going to be far more highly motivated to meet their work responsibilities. When an employee does not respond positively to being shown respect, then deep defensiveness is present and positive confrontation is required for the sake of all concerned, including the work organisation.

Enhancing relationship is about managers interacting with others in ways that elevate their self-esteem and their belief in themselves. This means that not only does there need to be the absence of destructive criticism, ridicule, comparisons, put-downs, impatience, aggression, harassment, cynicism or sarcasm, but the presence of unconditional regard, empathy, understanding, congruence, encouragement, support and expressed appreciation of work efforts and belief in each employee's potential. The manager also needs to send out a clear message to all employees that respectful relationships with one another are required and that any demeaning or threatening of any staff member will be regarded seriously. Such a declaration has to be supported by definite structures and procedures that make it possible and easy for an individual employee to take action on any neglect he/she experiences.

It is incumbent on managers to be watchful that there is not an unwritten rule that, arising from fear of retaliation, the workers fail to report the neglectful behaviour of fellow workers. It needs to be emphasised that such reporting is an act of maturity and courage and is necessary for the well-being of all members of staff, including those who perpetrate the neglect. Some form of sanction is required for those whose behaviour is a source of threat to the well-being of other employees. Sanctions are not punishments; they are necessary actions taken to vindicate the human rights that have been violated. It is integral to the manager's responsibility to enhance relationships, to explore positively and non-judgementally with the employee who perpetrated the violation the reasons for such neglectful responses. While two wrongs never make a right, an understanding and empathic approach may uncover an earlier and, perhaps, even greater experience of neglect on the part of the perpetrator.

This discovery does not mean that the current neglect is tolerated; on the contrary, the employee is requested to take responsibility for his/her defensive action and accept the sanction imposed. However, an opportunity needs to be provided for the employee to resolve the source of his/her neglectful behaviour. The most important sanction[1] is for the worker to apologise to his/her fellow worker and to commit to not repeating the offence. Once the violated right has been restored, no further sanctioning is required. However, the manager needs to maintain a close eye, to ensure that due action follows the spoken apology.

When the manager himself violates any of the rights of employees — physical, emotional, intellectual, social, creative, spiritual — he too needs to apologise and follow-through on corrective action. It is essential that there are established structures and procedures in place so that when a violation occurs, the employee can safely voice his/her distress and there is an onus on the manager to be accountable for the neglect perpetrated. An important challenge for all work organisations is to determine who it is monitors managers' relationships with employees. A common complaint among employees is the lack of systems and procedures to deal with managerial neglect. It is part of the brief of those who hold the reins of power in the organisation to take on this responsibility. Employees themselves, with the support of their trade unions, have, of course, a crucial role to play in ensuring that the appropriate procedures are in place.

   Those in higher management need to ensure that the nature of their relationships with those reporting to them is of an enhancing quality. When those at the top of the line are neglectful, the question arises as to who now is going to take them to task. To ensure accountability at all levels, an organisation has to be greater than the sum of its parts, but wise and mature leadership is required for this to happen. Of course, the ultimate sanction for the manager experiencing neglect from those above him is to resign and move on to a workplace that is worthy of his dignity.

---

1. My book *A Different Kind of Discipline* is relevant to this issue.

EMPOWERING AND ENABLING EMPLOYEES

The manager's task is not only to nurture but also to enable his staff members. Again he will require the back-up of the organisation to effectively manage this responsibility. Effective empowerment is based on the premise that each worker has immense potential and brings a unique giftedness to the workplace. It is the typical practice to evaluate people's potential through their educational achievements, but the street-wise manager knows that education is no index of maturity, creativity or commitment. Certainly, education does provide people with knowledge and skills, but it is their application that determines productivity. Individuals can be very efficient in what they do — they may do it perfectly — but yet not be especially effective because their perfectionism hampers the speed with which they can complete the task and it also blinkers their vision and openness to different ways of executing the job. The wise manager knows that a confident and dynamic worker is far more effective than the worker who lacks confidence and is slow to take a risk.

The core management task of building confidence is achieved through a process involving affirmation, encouragement, the setting of challenges, appreciation of specific attainments and the creation of opportunities for exploration of potential and giftedness.

A young man, speaking to me of his attempts to free himself of severe doubts about his capabilities, declared: 'belief is everything'. Yes, belief is everything; when you have a strong sense of your immense intelligence and unique giftedness, the world is your oyster. Unfortunately, owing to the confusion of intelligence with knowledge in homes, schools and elsewhere, many of us as children were judged as 'slow', 'weak', 'dumb', 'stupid', 'average', 'bright', 'highly intelligent' on the basis of the level of knowledge shown, particularly in the core subjects of reading, writing and arithmetic. Knowledge in any subject is an index of learning and opportunity, as well as motivation and the quality of the learning environment. Intelligence is the limitless potential to learn; science has shown that we use barely two per cent of the billions of brain cells we possess. A powerful boost to the confidence of an employee is to affirm his/her vast intelligence: 'I know you have all the ability to learn about this job and way beyond it.' Managers can also show belief in employees by listening to their viewpoints, asking their opinions and seeking their support in times of crisis.

It will help employees to maintain their confidence if the manager responds to mistakes and failures as opportunities for learning and not as a provocation for aggressive, critical and judgemental outbursts. When the work environment creates safety around failure, employees are far more adventurous and are quick to look for help when things go wrong. In workplaces where failure and mistakes are not tolerated, fear of being humiliated blocks risk-taking and leads to a covering up of mistakes or a blaming of others for them.

Encouragement means 'to give heart to' and it is the dynamic manager who breathes heart into employees' efforts by encouraging them and showing appreciation for their specific attainments. Generalised appreciation — 'you're great workers' — does not build confidence, but specific praise does: 'thank you for getting that order out to that client so efficiently.'

THE ART OF REFLECTION

Frequent reflection by managers on how they manage is a *sine qua non* of effective management. Reflection at the end of each work day provides the opportunity to review the managerial actions and decisions of the day and to identify those actions and decisions that were and were not progressive in nature. It is the mature manager who can admit mistakes, who can acknowledge that a different decision might have been more effective, and who can allow that certain interactions with staff need correcting or, at least, enhancing. The most urgent need for reflection is at those times when a manager engages in defensive responses.

The inside-out manager is well aware that the occasion of a defensive response is an opportunity to explore his own vulnerability and to resolve the hidden issue that lies behind the defensive response. The focus of the reflection is not directly on changing the defensive behaviour, but rather on the deeper underlying behaviour or attribute that is not being shown or expressed and which needs to be brought into the light. It is the realisation of what lies hidden that sets the manager on the road of mature and responsible behaviour again. For example, when a manager is impatient with an employee, he needs to reflect and ask the question, 'what is it that lies behind my impatience?' Possible causes are a sense of threat around expression of the right to fail, or insecurity about the fundamental human need for unconditional acceptance.

Managers also need to reflect on their own approach to work and whether or not they are doing the work they really want to do. There is nothing more soul-destroying than hating going to work every day. The manager is also wise to consider whether or not the work he does and the workplace are worthy of his dignity. Observation and reflection on how workers relate to him are critical. Furthermore, examination is required of the extent of the organisation's recognition of him as an individual and the level of support of his managerial role. The fact is that if managers sell out on themselves, they ultimately buy themselves a life of misery.

Reflection will certainly highlight the need for managers to undertake ongoing personal and interpersonal development and professional training in the understanding and management of what can be very complex human interactions.

SEEKING FEEDBACK ON MANAGEMENT STYLE

Sometimes the truth of how we are with others is first seen by others. This is particularly so for those managers who are not yet ready to see what they need to see. To feedback is to nurture, to let somebody know from a place of regard and respect what you feel and think about the relationship that lies between you. All management is about relationship and the manager who is open to knowing his employees and their experience of him has a glorious opportunity to build a real and open relationship with them. It is fascinating that many managers feel that it is okay for them to appraise their employees' carrying out of their work responsibilities, but do not see it as being equally necessary for employees to be given an opportunity to appraise the manager's ways of fulfilling his duties.

Indeed, it is not unusual for a manager to not see how threatening work appraisals can be for staff members themselves, but to become very sensitive when it is his turn to get feedback from workers on how they perceive his managing practices. When appraisals are a one-way street, they are experienced as threatening, rather than the nurturing and enabling exercise they could be when they become a process of feedback between equals with different levels of responsibility.

Whether sought informally or formally, the validity of the feedback will be largely dependent on how safe staff feel in relaying their authentic experiences of their interactions with the manager. Obviously, if staff members feel that their career prospects may be jeopardised or that victimisation may follow their honest feedback, then they are unlikely to provide genuine responses, either informally or formally. Verbal reassurance, backed up by policy and procedures, that such eventualities will not follow, is certainly required for honest expression to emerge.

There are certain work cultures where there is a non-stated, but nonetheless very powerful, proscription on questioning the policies, decisions and management style of the organisation and where there are little, or even no, opportunities for employees to voice their beliefs, values and grievances. This is an extremely unhealthy ethos, not only for the employees and the managers who conform to such a controlling approach, but for the long-term viability of the organisation. These organisations eventually implode, but only after a long, dark history of many people being hurt. When feedback is sought, the real test is the manager's own non-verbal, verbal and action responses to the feedback received, whether it be critical or positive. Some employees will be on the look-out for what they perceive to be weaknesses or deficiencies, but the mature employee also watches out for the manager's response to positive feedback. An exaggeratedly pleased response to positive feedback could reveal the manager's dependence on being seen as 'the best' or being liked; such dependence on the positive is likely to dry up necessary critical feedback and result in the employees' manipulation of the manager.

A common defence mechanism is hypersensitivity to criticism manifested by an aggressive response, or an upset or hurt reaction, or a silent withdrawal and consequent avoidance of employees, particularly those individuals who expressed the criticism. It is said that the best form of defence is attack and this is what the aggressive response to critical feedback is attempting to do. The ploy is to distract attention from the manager's own behaviour and to make it less likely that an employee will express criticism again. The problem here is that the presence of the defensive responses means that mature communication has broken down and the critical issues that require resolution will not now be considered.

A further confounding factor is the employee's reaction to the manager's defensive responses; when this, in turn, is defensive, there is no chance of resolution. One of the great challenges for a manager is to learn the art of separateness (see below) so that he can truly hear what an employee expresses, whether positive or critical, as being totally about that employee's met or unmet needs. The responsibility of the manager is to identify both met and unmet needs, and to capitalise on the former and work harder to meet the latter, once these are realistic.

A not uncommon defensive response to positive feedback is to dismiss it, dilute it or neutralise it. The threat underlying the defensive response may be that 'more will be asked of me if I acknowledge the present achievement'. Another possible source of the underlying threat in positive feedback is that it may threaten a defensive self-concept of 'being your average man'. When the dismissal is extreme — 'don't talk rubbish' — it suggests that even deeper issues of personal unworthiness may be present. Diluting positive feedback is not dissimilar to dismissing it, but it is softer; for example, 'isn't it my job?' or 'there's no need for that' or 'sure you're great yourself'. Neutralising positive feedback takes the heart out of what has been said: 'it's nothing really' or 'a man's got to do what a man's got to do' or 'don't go all soft on me now'. Whatever defensive response to positive feedback may be exhibited, the manager needs to be aware that his defensiveness is likely to lead to employees stepping back into their own defensive ways, thereby blocking progress in creating an open, mature and accountable work ethos.

Creating effective ways for its managers to seek feedback on their management style is the responsibility of the work organisation. Ways of ensuring that the manager carries out the prescribed practices in mature ways is a necessary development. The worker-manager appraisal system — informal and formal — is best designed by the workers themselves, in consultation with the manager. When a manager does not act upon the given feedback, a back-up system to ensure that the employees are heard is required.

UNDERSTANDING HUMAN BEHAVIOUR

Understanding human behaviour in itself does not guarantee effective management, but it certainly is a key factor; managers need to understand that all human behaviour is meaningful, no matter how difficult, extreme or bizarre[2] it may appear to be. Without insight into human behaviour, a manager cannot respond in the workplace in ways that are wise and progressive. Managers who perceive and judge and label challenging behaviour as, for example, 'bad', 'downright blackguarding', 'thuggish', 'delinquent', 'revengeful', 'out to get me' cannot make progress with the employees who manifest the defensive behaviour so described. It is necessary that the manager understands the wisdom and meaning of his own challenging behaviours before he is in a position to appreciate the wisdom in the behaviour of others.

There is no suggestion here that understanding a challenging behaviour means having to tolerate it. On the contrary, confrontation (see below) is expedient because, no matter what the underlying reasons or the hidden intention of the behaviour, it cannot be allowed to threaten the welfare of others or the aims of the organisation. But the confrontation that comes from understanding the meaning of the defensive behaviour is very different to confrontation that arises from judgement and labelling. The latter only

---

2. My book *The Power of 'Negative' Thinking* examines this topic in detail.

exacerbates the defensive responses, whereas the former opens up the possibility of resolution.

Identifying the underlying sources of a challenging behaviour and the subconscious intention of the behaviour are distinct processes. An example will clarify the two-dimensional ingenious process involved. Take timidity as an example of a challenging behaviour. The source of the particular worker's timidity could lie in experiences of being frequently and heavily intimidated by a parent and/or teacher in early childhood and his/her wise inner emotional conclusion at that time that 'it is not safe for me to take risks or express what I need or feel'. Wise child! However, the *intention* of the timidity also requires seeing, because while the source lies in the past, the intention continues into the present time.

The true purpose of the timidity is to offset any further possibility of being intimidated here and now in the workplace: 'if I don't make myself visible then I won't attract your attention.' A manager may judge a worker who shows timidity as 'having no back-bone' or as 'incapable of standing up for herself' or as 'weak-kneed'. Such judgements are reflective of the manager's low level of maturity and reveal his lack of understanding of the psychological wisdom of timidity. In truth, individuals who are passive, shy or timid are 'standing up for themselves' in the only way possible for them when they were defenceless in the face of authority figures whose defensive behaviours were major sources of threat to their well-being.

The manager who understands the wise process involved can create the safety in his relationship with the employee that will allow the employee to experiment with expressing what has lain hidden for many years — his/her individuality, viewpoints, feelings and needs. When the employee begins, over time, to experience the physical, emotional, social and intellectual safety that the wise manager provides, he/she will move towards being authentic and assertive and gradually drop the defensive responses of timidity. Of course, the ultimate responsibility for the timidity lies with the employee, but a mature, wise and supportive manager can be the lifeline that enables the employee to start on his/her own pursuit of freedom from fear.

Take conformity as a further example for examining the two-dimensional process involved in understanding defensive behaviour. There is a great difference between conformity and co-operation: conformity is an outside-in defensive response to the demands of others, whereas co-operation is an inside-out open and chosen response. Behind conformity lie the dark forces of unworthiness, resentment, suppressed anger and sometimes rage that seriously limit commitment, creativity, dynamism and achievement. Behind co-operation lies the solid ground of possession of self that manifests itself in responsible and mature work commitment, creativity, dynamism, high attainment and decision-making. The source of conformity will lie in the remote past where you dared not be different, and may still be present in a working environment that is threatening. The intention of conformity is to not 'rock the boat' or 'ruffle the feathers' of authority figures because the likelihood is high of being demeaned or lessened in some way or other: 'if I'm the same as you, then surely you can't reject me.' The intention of co-operation is genuineness and authenticity in relating to others and carrying out work responsibilities.

The ability to understand that there is an underlying source and a wise intention to all behaviour, particularly challenging behaviour, is a skill that no manager can do without. It is an understanding that is not easily attained, not because of its complexity, but because it entails the manager taking the risk of being self-reflective and figuring out the sources and intentions of his own behaviours. Looking into the mirror of our own defensive responses is highly challenging because, at times, it means having to make difficult decisions that others who are in defensive places themselves will be sorely threatened by. In order to learn this skill of understanding human behaviour, managers require training and all the support they can muster within the organisation, particularly from the top down. It is the dark organisation that does not provide resources and support for the emergence of wisdom and understanding.

THE ART OF STAYING SEPARATE

If being able to understand the sources and the intention of defensive behaviour is crucial to effective management, so too is the ability to stay separate when such behaviours are exhibited. At an intrapersonal level, separateness is about keeping your person separate from your work. The manager who is dependent on his work because he identifies himself with it cannot maturely lead others. The paradox is that the more separate his identity is from his work, the more effective is the manager.

In the interpersonal domain, separateness is the wisdom of seeing that the other person's behaviour, even though it may appear to be directed at you, is totally about that person. Personalising another person's behaviour as saying something about you leads to an immediate breakdown in communication or, more accurately, to a recourse to defensive communication. It is not difficult to imagine that when a manager becomes enmeshed with an employee's behaviour and perceives it as an attempt to 'get at him' or make life difficult for him, he is not in a solid position to sort out the problem. For example, if an employee shows hostility when a manager makes a request and the manager reacts by bawling out the employee, he has not managed the difficult situation, even though that is what he is being paid to do. He could also react by going silent and being determined never to ask anything of that employee again but to 'sure as hell make life difficult for him'. He may begin to ignore and gossip about this staff member and block any possibilities of career progress.

With all these defensive reactions, the manager has lost sight of the issue at hand and there is an urgency for him to reflect on his responses. What is required is that he sees that the employee's initial hostile response was completely about the employee, and his job as manager is to enhance the relationship by remaining separate and attempting to discover what lies behind the hostile response and what is its intention. It is easier to enhance relationship when there is co-operation; the real test for a manager is to do it in the face of non-co-operation, particularly when it is of a hostile nature. What then could the manager have done? Internally, he needed to remind himself of the reality that the employee's behaviour is about himself/herself and to respond to him/her from that separate position. Such a response would take the form of an enquiry: 'John, I'm wondering what your hostile response to my request is all about.'

This response effectively puts the ball back in the employee's court, because only John knows the real message that lies hidden behind the defensive response. There is no guarantee that the manager's mature response will immediately get back a mature answer. What is more likely is another hostile reaction: 'what are you talking about?' (said aggressively). Again, the manager needs to hold his solid place of separateness and respond: 'I am concerned to know what is the difficulty for you in doing what I've requested?' By staying separate, the manager creates the safety for the employee to be open. The employee may now respond and say, 'I'm up to my eyeballs with work at the moment and your request is putting me under more pressure.' There may still be an 'edge' to his voice tone, but at least now the manager knows the employee's position and they have a chance to negotiate the situation.

The other side of the coin of separateness is the recognition that whatever the manager himself thinks, feels, says or does is totally about him. It is incumbent on managers to completely own their own responses and not project responsibility for themselves on to workers. The manager who describes his staff as 'a bunch of shysters' is far removed from any sense of being separate and owning his own needs and ambition. What lies behind the manager's judgement of his staff is an unspoken need for co-operation and commitment. The likelihood is that his staff have no sense of what he really wishes of them and his critical attitude has triggered defensiveness on their part. This is an important issue to see: when workers do not stay separate from the manager's defensive responses, a cycle of defensive relating takes over and a tense and difficult work ethos emerges. It now becomes a situation where you have the blind leading the blind.

It might appear that separateness is difficult when it comes to dealing with the defensive behaviour of another, but it can be even more difficult to stay separate from the affirming responses of another. It follows that if difficult behaviours are completely about the person engaging in them, then the same must be true for positive responses. For instance, if an employee communicates to his/her manager that 'you're a great man to work for' and the manager hears that as being about him, and not about the worker, he now becomes enmeshed with the worker's positive view of his management. In truth, the worker's positive appraisal reveals that his needs are being met by the manager and that he/she is pleased about this. Certainly, the manager can enjoy the fact that this employee has a sense of fulfilment and be pleased that he has contributed to it.

However, another worker may not have the same experience — remember each employee has a different manager — and what then is the manager to believe? By staying separate he is able to evaluate the experiences of each worker and respond uniquely to each person's situation. To the employee who is positive he can respond: 'I'm happy you enjoy working with me' and to the employee who is discontented: 'I'd like to discover what is causing you to feel discontented and how we can work together to resolve that situation for you.' It is for the manager himself to know himself and to evaluate and continually reflect on his own style of management. When a manager becomes dependent on positive feedback from employees, he may find it very difficult to make the tough decisions that are sometimes necessary.

A legitimate question to pose here is: why would a manager need to ask for feedback on his management style when what employees say is about themselves? The answer is that feedback provides the opportunity for employees to communicate whether or not the work they do and the workplace (which includes management) is worthy of their dignity. When management style is neglectful in nature, inevitably the dignity of employees is under threat and the opportunities need to be provided for such neglect to be voiced.

THE ART OF CONFRONTATION

There are three key situations that call for confrontation on the part of the manager:

- ☐ when the manager's own defensive behaviour is a source of threat to the well-being of others and the aims of the organisation
- ☐ when the defensive behaviours of staff members are a source of threat to the manager's well-being, other staff members and the needs of the organisation

□ when the organisation (in the persons of those who hold the reins of power) is not respectful of the rights of workers, of the manager and of organisational progress

Failure to confront any of the above situations means that a manager is not fulfilling his primary purpose of enhancing relationships. The consequences of the omission of confrontation are that the dis-ease in the work environment, like an untreated wound, will deepen and fester, leading to an unhealthy work ethos. Confrontation must not be confused with aggression; the manager who attacks himself, staff members or the organisation will only deepen the wound of unmet needs. Likewise, when a manager approaches the problem in a way that blames himself or the workers, no progress is possible. If the manner in which the problem is approached is defensive in any way, then defence is meeting defence, and all that happens is that more defensiveness ensues.

Confrontation by its very nature is an act of caring. Its purpose is to restore equilibrium so that individuals have felt actively listened to, understood and championed and see that unmet needs are met or are in the process of being met. Confrontation involves real and open responses that lead to the resolution of a conflict.

The manager who manages from the inside out is much more likely to be authentic and caring in confronting an untenable situation.

When it comes to challenging defensive responses, on the part of an individual or a group of workers, the manager needs to take the following steps:

□ ensure that the confrontation takes place in a safe and private setting
□ provide an assurance of confidentiality

□ state the preference that the issue in hand is resolved at this level within the organisation
□ employ direct and clear communication
□ maintain separateness no matter what the reaction to the confrontation.

In confronting the target behaviour, the manager is best starting from a position of seeking to understand its meaning and intention. Starting from this position, he avoids slipping into being judgemental, which would quickly dry up any possibility of resolution. Take as an example the situation where the manager has received a complaint from a staff member about being harassed by a supervisor and he now has to confront this supervisor. After the manager has thanked the supervisor for coming to the meeting, he prefaces his intended enquiry with the assurance of confidentiality and the preference that the matter to be discussed be resolved between them and not have to be taken higher up the hierarchy of power.

He then states directly (addressing the supervisor by his/her preferred title) and clearly what the matter is ('a complaint of harassment has been made against you and I wish to hear your side of the story'). The manager elaborates on the complaint and observes closely the supervisor's non-verbal responses to what he is saying. When he invites the supervisor's verbal response, he wants to see if there is congruence or incongruence between the non-verbal and verbal responses, but holds his observations until an appropriate time in the discussion. The supervisor may well go into defence and want to know immediately, 'who made the complaint?' How this question is asked — tone of voice, facial expression, nature of eye contact (if any), body posture, body movements — are important indicators of the degree of defensiveness present.

Whatever the response is, the manager states the name of the staff member and invites the supervisor to give his/her side of the story.

All sorts of possible answers may emerge at this stage. The supervisor may:

□ blame self ('she's right, I was impatient, under-pressure')
□ blame the staff member ('he's always complaining; he tries to get away with murder')
□ blame the organisation ('what do you expect when this place keeps making more and more demands on me?'; 'targets have to be met, don't they?')
□ blame the manager ('you don't give me enough back-up'; 'you don't see half of what's happening')
□ take responsibility ('Sheila is correct; I did shout at her and I understand that this is not acceptable behaviour').

When the supervisor admits responsibility, resolution of the threatening behaviour is straightforward. When the supervisor resorts to one or more of the defensive responses, he/she is not yet ready to face the reality of the interactions with the staff member.

The manager has two challenges now – to continue to champion the rights of the employee who has made the complaint and to understand and attempt to get behind the supervisor's defences.

He could respond in a way that addresses both challenges: 'Michael, I hear your frustrations with Sheila (or with me or with the organisation) and later I would like to discuss these with you but, right now, I want us to resolve what has occurred between you and Sheila.' The response here might be: 'I didn't mean any harm; she doesn't have to be so hypersensitive.' A positive movement has emerged, though clouded with a defensive one. Taking account of this, the manager might now respond: 'Whatever about Sheila's hypersensitivity, I am glad to hear that it was not your intention to cause any harm. Tell me what was your intention'; to which question, the supervisor might say: 'to get the job done'.

Again taking account of what the supervisor is saying, the manager goes on: 'Michael, I'm aware of your commitment to achieving targets, but this has to be done in a way that is supportive rather than threatening to a staff member's welfare.' Michael's response, at this point, might be: 'I apologise. What do you wish me to do?' To which the manager replies: 'Precisely what you have done here and that is to apologise to Sheila. I would also like to return to the frustrations you expressed earlier and look at how these can be resolved for you.'

It is important that the manager ensures that the supervisor follows through on the action agreed and that the staff member who experienced the harassment is commended for his/her assertiveness and reassured that any further experience of intimidation will be taken even more seriously.

In the scene depicted above, it can be seen that the manager maintained separateness from the supervisor's defensive responses by sticking to the issue that needed resolution, while acknowledging the possible unmet needs of the supervisor. Communication would have broken down if he had introjected (internalised) any of the supervisor's defensive responses and responded by defending Sheila, himself and the organisation. Staying separate is essential to effective confrontation and conflict resolution.

If the supervisor had denied the allegation: 'I don't know what you're talking about' or 'whoever reported this is just out to cause trouble', the manager would have had a more serious challenge on hand. If he is a manager who knows his supervisors, he is likely to have a fair idea of whether or not the allegation is true. Nonetheless, the supervisor's denial cannot be allowed to block progress on the staff relationship issue. His response to the supervisor's denial could take the form: 'Michael, I hear your denial, but I need now to set up an investigation because I have two different stories about what happened. I would appreciate your co-operation in resolving this issue and I will request the same co-operation of Sheila. Furthermore, until this problem is resolved, I will organise for Sheila to be assigned to another supervisor.'

Michael may relent at this point or he may further dig his heels in. Whatever the response of the supervisor, the manager needs to ensure that he follows through on the investigation — for everybody's sake!

When the organisation itself needs to be confronted by the manager, the situation can become quite challenging. Some work organisations threaten serious consequences if a manager persists in being assertive and non-conformist. The threats he may be exposed to include ridicule, anonymity, demotion, loss of job. Difficult decisions are called for in the face of such controlling forces. Sometimes, what is needed is the decision to resign from such a dark organisation. It does no good for your well-being to compromise your dignity and your authenticity.

Healthy organisations welcome confrontation, whether it is from the top down or bottom up. Creating safety for confrontation will ensure that a wellness cycle is maintained, leading to a contented workforce and a maximisation of the organisation's potential.

THE IMPORTANCE OF BOUNDARIES

A clear distinction needs to be made between a boundary and a defence. A defence is a behaviour that hides some aspect of self that you are fearful of showing and reflects the kind of neglectful relationship you have learned to develop with yourself, with others and with the world, including work. On the other hand, a boundary is an active determination to be real, authentic and expressive of who you truly are. In establishing a boundary, you stand firm in being true to self and in this way 'you cannot be false to any man'. Being real is the hardest challenge of all, particularly when the ethos of a work organisation is defensive and controlling. However, when a manager does not stay steadfast to his real self, to his true beliefs and values, he lets himself down, along with his staff members and, ironically, the organisation.

In all his interactions, preferably in and out of work — physical, sexual, emotional, intellectual, behavioural, social, creative and spiritual — a manager needs to establish definite and clear boundaries around what is respectful and affirming of self and others. Whilst he will attempt to understand the defensive behaviours of others, he will not collude with them, but will send out strong messages of what he expects of himself, for himself and of others and for others. He remains non-judgemental, but does not tolerate neglectful actions toward self and others and will always take action to resolve any neglect experienced. It is by his actions that a person's defensiveness is manifested; it is equally true that it is by actions that a person's boundaries around being true to self and others are manifested.

Giving in 'for the sake of peace and quiet' is a common defensive response of the manager who leads from the outside in. This in turn leads to an absence of boundaries. The 'peace and quiet' are pseudo, because true peace and quiet are the products of realness, genuineness and fearlessness.

Whilst solid boundaries are necessary, unless managers are vigilant they can become rigid. Rigid boundaries are actually defensive in nature. Solidity and permeability of boundaries may be required at certain times. The reason for this is that relationships in the workplace are not best served by rigid laws, but by respect, understanding and compassion. In other words, people are more important than rules. For example, a manager who has a strong boundary around his legitimate wish for workers to be on time for work may be called upon to show flexibility. If he is family-friendly, his boundary will be permeable so as to permit a mother (or father) to get their children to school before coming to work at a time beyond the norm. Permeable boundaries do not mean being soft, as the manager will expect the staff member to make up the time lost in an arranged and agreed way.

CHAPTER 7

MANAGING FROM THE OUTSIDE IN

DEFENSIVE MANAGEMENT STYLES

Style of management will largely be a function of the extent to which a manager knows self and staff members. Knowledge, skill and competence also play a part, as does the ethos of the organisation. Managers who are highly defensive automatically manage from the outside in because their defence involves controlling forces outside of themselves which they perceive as threats to their inner well-being. Any form of defensive management is a block to the progress of the manager himself, of employees and of the organisation.

There are very few managers who are not real and authentic in some aspects of their functioning, and in these ways of relating considerable progress may occur. When the manager experiences threat in specific aspects of functioning and hides this sense of threat, there will be a block to progress. It is incumbent on organisations to have selection systems that not only evaluate the career record of a manager, but also evaluate the potential candidate's level of emotional and social maturity. Emotional and social maturity is concerned with how the manager sees himself, how he interacts with others, his basic concept of managing and how he views his work. Observation, direct interaction and feedback from previous employers, rather than the psychometric tests so often used, are the most reliable means of collecting data on these essential aspects of management. The data gained from

90

direct experience cannot be bettered by tests, no matter how developed these are.

Organisations that have reinforced defensive management styles may find the more direct and personal means of obtaining information on candidates somewhat threatening, and the selection personnel in such organisations are unlikely to go against the prevailing defensive ethos for fear of jeopardising their own positions. Work organisations whose ethos is primarily defensive usually have a hierarchical management structure, and change in the organisation is likely to happen only from the top down. The most pressurised group within this hierarchical structure is the middle management group.

While the nature of defensive management will reflect the personal and interpersonal defences employed by the particular manager in his everyday living, it is possible to identify some common defensive styles:

- managers who *make* things happen
- managers who *let* things happen
- managers who *do not know* what is happening
- managers who have to have everything *perfect*
- managers who *do not care* what is happening
- managers who *placate* to get things to happen
- managers who are single-minded and who *lose sight* of what is happening.

MANAGERS WHO *MAKE* THINGS HAPPEN

These managers are often described as 'heroic'; as people who 'kick ass', 'wipe the board clean', 'take no nonsense', 'have all the answers'; people whom others 'dare not question'. These are the managers who 'give heart attacks', but, ironically, never expect to get one themselves. Apparently, the human heart has the potential to last for 400 years, but such managers can destroy their hearts within 40 years. They operate totally from the head, and view feelings as 'soft stuff'. They dominate and control, they command, they can be vicious in giving feedback, and they pressurise for results, results, results. They have no concept that people matter. Their whole focus is on profitability. They tend to be utterly careless about their own physical and psycho-social well-being and show little or no concern for the well-being of employees. Their management style is not considerate of the person, family or marriage. Their attitude is, 'if you can't take the heat, then get out of the kitchen'. If they can, they will fire people at will or, without consultation, demote employees or transfer them to difficult assignments.

These managers are unapproachable, unavailable and have no knowledge of how to enhance relationships in the workplace. They can sometimes achieve remarkable results in the short term, but in the long term they are a liability to an organisation. They give no consideration to the cost of their policies in human terms. Inevitably, their style of defensive management creates low staff morale and employees begin to find ways to defend themselves against the enormous threats to the self and to career that this type of management raises. Staff turnover, absenteeism, sickness, resistance, cliques that can informally attempt to undermine the manager's position, are some of the effects this management style provokes. Resentment, revenge, rage, anger, fear, passivity, timidity, gossip, back-biting, sabotage, blame, rigidity, non-cooperation are but some of the defensive reactions that employees manifest in the face of this type of defensive management.

Managers who *make* things happen have totally enmeshed their sense of self with their work and are utterly dependent on success as a means of gaining recognition from others. Because their sense of worth is not separate from what they do, they are not in a position to treat workers with respect and to communicate in ways that are open, clear, direct and equal. Conflict issues and problems are seen as threats, rather than challenges for which there is an infinity of solutions. These managers tend to have an extremely unbalanced lifestyle; they work long hours, are first in and last out of the workplace; they neglect self, marriage and family, but will rationalise that they are 'doing all this for the family'.

It is a neglect of the manager, the employees and the organisation itself when such a management style is not confronted. Confrontation is an act of caring, an act of responsibility; an act that requires explicit and confidential structures to implement. The manager himself needs to be provided with opportunities to understand and free himself of his defences either within or outside the organisation.

MANAGERS WHO *LET* THINGS HAPPEN

The source of this kind of management is the manager's own doubts about self. His passivity is clever and his tendency is to pass on to others the buck of responsibility for what needs to happen, because it means he does not take any risks, but he expects the employee to take the risks he will not take himself. When anything goes wrong, he will blame the employees, but will not reflect on his own contribution. He is happy to take all the credit when things go right.

From the organisation's point of view, this management style is disastrous because of the lack of real leadership. This type of management is like a boat without a rudder which can get into choppy waters, or hit calm waters, be beached on a sandy island, smash upon the rocks or drift way out to sea and become totally lost. Because there is no leadership or supervision of employees' time-keeping, work efforts and interrelationships, all sorts of ill-practices evolve. Motivation, too, will plummet because this manager, while he may be approachable, is not available in terms of active listening, problem-solving, creativity, initiative and drive. Neither does this manager affirm the presence of employees or praise and recognise work attainments. It is a desert-like style of management and there are no oases. Productivity greatly suffers. Motivation, drive, creativity and initiative all dry up. Pilfering and carelessness around equipment and products are common results of this management style.

This manager sees work responsibilities as a source of threat. His sense of self is enmeshed with work in the same way as with the manager who makes things happen, but the difference is that he employs the defence of avoidance of responsibilities as his way of reducing threat, whereas the manager who dominates employs the defence of endless drive towards success, success, success.

The manager who lets things happen requires confrontation as much as the *heroic* manager. Even though it may appear that the heroic management style creates more havoc in terms of human relationships, staff morale and creativity, passivity is just as neglectful of people and seriously blocks mature work practices. Managers who lead from the inside out are champions of the rights of workers, the rights of the organisation and their own rights. Neither the *heroic* nor the *passive* type of management displays any championing of their own and other people's rights.

MANAGERS WHO *DO NOT KNOW* WHAT IS HAPPENING

These managers are just not there; they may be out on the golf course or away at this conference or that meeting or arrive late and leave early. They have no sense of their own presence and, therefore, cannot affirm the presence of others. It is as if their defensive absence from their own self is projected on to their work responsibilities. Avoidance and being absent are powerful ways of not having to deal with reality. This type of management is more common in family-run businesses where offspring who were 'spoilt' as children now, as adults, have no sense of how to take charge. They have protectively come to believe that the world revolves around them and that they do not need to know what is happening. Children who are overprotected are deprived of the opportunities of becoming 'response-able'; the sense of one's capability is the foundation stone to being responsible.

Businesses run in such a style collapse quickly. It is not that the manager wants this to happen; it is that he does not know how to stop it from happening. To actually address his incapability for responsibility would mean having to confront a parent who did everything for him and, thereby, kept him totally helpless. To be real, to confront this situation, would mean risking rejection from this parent; it would also mean facing the enormity of his vulnerability. Not an easy task!

One of the problems with family businesses is that there are rarely any back-up structures to deal with neglect. Staff who work in family businesses can be at high risk, because nobody is willing to call a spade a spade. Whisperings go on, gossip, covert complaining, but rarely is direct action taken. Staff turnover becomes high, sickness and absenteeism frequent and business progress becomes slow or static.

Of course this type of management is not peculiar to family-run businesses; it can also be exhibited by the manager who becomes involved in too many projects. His tendency is to be dynamic and creative but he is more like the 'butterfly' who flits from flower to flower, rather than the 'busy bee' who gets down to the work that has to be done and stays with the one flower. Organisations can often be tempted to promote to a managerial position a member who has shown creativity and inventiveness. But these employees are not always disposed to take on managerial responsibilities and are likely to continue to pursue their compulsion to be different and creative. When an employee's identity is tied up with being different and creative, it is best for the organisation to find a position for him/her that taps into that drive to find visibility through creativity. However, the organisation needs to be wary of exploiting the employee's vulnerability for its own gain; a time will come when the lack of real care will boomerang.

MANAGERS WHO HAVE TO HAVE EVERYTHING *PERFECT*

May organisations be delivered from *perfectionists* who are poor at leadership and eventually burn out. If the *make things happen* manager is addicted to success, so too is the manager who is perfectionistic, but the perfectionist attempts to achieve this goal through putting extreme pressure on self rather than directly on others. 'Success' is not an accurate term in this situation because such a manager is far from successful in how he relates to employees, life-partner, children and friends. Striving to have everything right drives this manager to untold neglect of self, marriage, family, friendships and it destroys his sense of adventure.

His perfectionistic style is a mirror for this manager of the extent to which he has had to hide his deep human needs to explore, to experiment, to fail, to succeed, to be free to be self.

The manager who employs the defence of perfectionism has learned that the only way to offset personal pain and interpersonal disappointment is do everything oneself, and never to rely on another. For this reason, he has huge difficulty in delegating responsibilities and, when he does, he struggles with letting the employee get on with the work, and he tends to continually check on progress. The over-supervision can undermine the confidence of the employees. This manager does not provide feedback to staff and he reserves the kudos for all attainments for himself. He is too intense to be approachable and too involved with his work to be available. Encouragement of work efforts and affirmation of the self of staff do not feature in his management style because these are not responses he shows to himself.

MANAGERS WHO *DO NOT CARE* WHAT IS HAPPENING

This type of management is unlikely to operate in large organisations but can flourish in small businesses or family-run businesses. Usually this manager has a huge 'chip on his shoulder' and blames the world for everything unpleasant that has happened to him. He feels that the world owes him and that he is damned if he is going to give of himself to a world that has let him down. Everything he does is done with resentment, and his attitude to staff is dismissive and aggressive. He is stuck in a vicious cycle of blaming everyone, who in turn blame back or retreat from him, which confirms his worst fear that people are just out to 'get' him or let him down. The frequency, intensity and endurance of his 'don't care' attitude and behaviour are important determinants of the detrimental effects on his own psycho-social well-being, staff morale and managerial effectiveness.

Because his main defence is projection (the blaming of others), he will lack any understanding, empathy or compassion for the difficulties of staff. He will see their vulnerabilities as weaknesses and he may well be quite cruel in his verbal responses to workers. He really does not care about anything or anybody because he feels nobody cares for him. He may be alcohol- or drug-dependent and these addictions may lead to him exhausting the financial resources of the business. This manager is in serious need of professional psycho-social help and any staff member who passively or aggressively colludes with his neglectful behaviour also needs to seek help.

MANAGERS WHO *PLACATE* TO GET THINGS TO HAPPEN

The placation of employees must not be confused with the enhancement of relationships or the enablement of employees. The purpose of enhancing is to foster staff relationships that are respectful, mature, equal and dynamic in nature. The aim of enabling is to help employees believe in their own capability and to provide opportunities for them to explore their giftedness and potential. Managers who placate fail to exercise these two fundamental aspects of management. Placating is a defensive way of attempting to get employees to take on their responsibilities and to adopt the manager's vision of how the organisation can be most effective. Placating is a manipulation, a bending over backwards to please employees in order to get co-operation.

The manager who placates possesses little positive sense of self. He manages from the outside in to the extent that he believes he has to foster co-operation through over-praising, pleasing, exaggerated gratitude, even begging. He may be 'successful' with employees who will 'feel sorry for him', but there will be employees who will perceive him as being 'spineless' and 'weak' and will take full advantage of that 'weakness'. There is no real leadership here; work is likely to be done at the whim of employees. Some employees will come and go as they please, take long breaks, and arrive for work late and leave early. They will shrug off any attempt by the manager to encourage them to be responsible because they know he will take no definite action on their tardiness.

It may appear that this manager is considerate of the person, relationships and family, but his consideration will be rightly seen as manipulative and it will not be trusted. Mature relationships can be formed only from a place of realness; they do not develop from a place of defensiveness. While this manager may be very approachable — he poses no visible threat — he is not truly available because he finds it difficult to make the 'hard' decisions. Employees will not have confidence in this manager to take strong action. Those employees who exploit his vulnerability may approach this manager, but it will be to meet their own ends and not the ends of the organisation.

MANAGERS WHO ARE SINGLE-MINDED AND WHO *LOSE SIGHT* OF WHAT IS HAPPENING

This manager will have his sight on only one ball and that is likely to be the ball of productivity. His vision of management is confined to that one goal and he can totally miss seeing that his relationships with staff are poor, even disabling, that staff morale is low and that employees 'hate his guts'. This manager emerges from his office or has meetings in his office only to check progress on targets. He has no sense of being considerate towards the person, relationship and family; no sense of the importance of treating staff members as individuals; no insight into the sometimes troubled worlds of his staff. He rarely reflects on his own life and may miss the difficulties in his own marriage and family. He is ambitious and dependent on work to sustain him.

He differs from the manager who makes things happen because he does not tend to be aggressive and dominant and is obsessive or overtly neglectful of staff. It is more the case that his single-mindedness blinds him to any other reality and he relentlessly keeps his focus on the achievement of productivity targets. He is largely emotionless and may have come from an emotionless family, where a work ethic was the only important family value. This manager is often referred to as managing from an ivory tower because he makes no real contact with employees.

This manager can be very highly skilled in his field, but he lacks any interpersonal skills. An organisation may feel it is fortunate to have such a dedicated manager, but his style of leadership will lead to all sorts of relationship and morale difficulties. He will not be perceived as available or approachable.

The greatest concern here is the manager's emotionless and mechanistic approach to living; he is 'all head' but possesses no 'heart'. Even though occupationally successful, he lives in an emotional desert and, if married with children, he will have serious relationship difficulties. In many ways, he is terrified of intimacy and he fills that void with work, work, work. He requires in-depth psychotherapeutic help to resolve the childhood sources of his emotionless state. He may be a high suicide risk and, certainly, a high health risk.

Because he dedicates his life to the organisation, any attempt by somebody higher in rank to confront his style of management will be perceived as an act of betrayal. He is so locked into being the organisation's man, it can be utterly devastating if he is confronted, demoted, sidelined or requested to stand down. It is as if the organisation is the family he never had; he will perceive any criticism as indicating that he is not being good enough and he may plummet into deep depression.

CHAPTER 8

MANAGING COMMUNICATION

COMMUNICATING FROM THE INSIDE OUT

Effective and mature communication is not a technique you can learn; the way you communicate arises automatically from how you see yourself. A solid sense of self and a consequent separateness from and independence of others is the cornerstone of effective communication. You may attempt to practise what you perceive or have been taught as 'positive' ways of communicating, but the non-verbal accompaniments will betray you if the foundation of a mature relationship with self is not present.

Eighty per cent of communication is non-verbal and while some of this can be 'put on' (in the same way as verbal communication), most non-verbal manifestations spring spontaneously from the shaky or solid ground of the individual's interior life. We have all encountered the over-hearty handshake and the false smile, and we may have encountered such pretence in ourselves. Congruence involves consistency between what you say in words and in body language. Tone and speed of voice, verbal emphasis, facial expression, body posture, eye contact are what indicate the authenticity of what is said. Because what we express outwardly reflects how we are in ourselves, all communication is essentially about getting through to self. The person who speaks from a place of inner conviction and confidence has no need to persuade others, but is willing to express his/her own truth and allow the listeners to come to their own conclusions about what he/she has expressed.

The person who communicates from the inside out knows that the attempt 'to get through' to another is not communication, but an attempt to control. Mature communication is about being true to one's own beliefs and convictions and being willing to allow others to express what is true for them. Only in such an equal and non-persuasive space can true mutual listening occur and the possibility for understanding and fair negotiation on differences be achieved.

The manager who communicates from the inside out is truly appreciative of difference, no matter how much it diverges from his own convictions. He knows that no truth is cast in stone and it is the listening to and appreciation of difference that leads to a widening and deepening of truth. Where difference remains on a particular issue, following respectful listening, understanding, appreciation and negotiation, the manager who is confident and mature will not impose his will but will seek a mutually agreed action that can test the reality of different views expressed.

This may mean choosing an option that tests out the viability of an opposing viewpoint and, at a later stage, a similar opportunity for the other viewpoint. Certainly, there are situations, e.g. situations involving physical and sexual safety, a productivity deadline, bullying and absenteeism where, in spite of differences, a manager may need to initiate a definite course of action. But this needs to be executed in a manner that does not in any way disrespect the person or the viewpoint of the protagonists. Indeed, following the 'emergency', further discussion on the prevailing differences needs to be programmed and not forgotten.

COMMUNICATING FROM THE OUTSIDE IN

The manager who communicates from the outside in is dogged by doubts about what he says or does, about his own beliefs and values. This manager attempts to persuade others to accept his viewpoint and, when such persuasion does not work, may resort to verbal aggression or manipulative sulking or threats. The challenge with the manager who uses communication as an act of control is that he attempts to gain inner conviction through persuading others, rather than through reflection.

The manager who communicates from the outside in has little tolerance for difference and misses the potential that such differences can offer an organisation. This manager is unlikely to seek the opinions of others or may 'play at' seeking employees' views, but his intention will be to impose his own viewpoints. Such communication piles up difficulties in relationships for this manager; those involved with him may react with defensive responses, such as resentment, resistance, conformity, formation of informal oppositional cliques, passivity and the drying up of creative expression.

Of course, this manager will defensively be convinced that his way of communicating is what employees need and will perceive understanding and respect for difference as not belonging to the 'real' world. The challenge with such a manager is that he is not in a position to be able to take feedback on his style of communication, certainly not from the bottom up. He is more likely to 'correct' his ways when feedback comes from the top down; however, true change towards communication that is congruent and authentic will come only from the manager's realisation of his own worth, value and convictions.

Another clever form of communication from the outside in is passive communication, whereby the manager allows the employees to take the lead and, when things go wrong, he can always blame the workers.

The mature work organisation ensures that there are back-up systems to deal with the situation where employees encounter a manager who communicates from the outside in. The absence of such systems can mean that employees are condemned to a very difficult work environment and, indeed, the manager is condemned to remaining 'stuck' in non-effective means of communication. An unhappy atmosphere, absenteeism, staff turnover and low productivity figures are the typical results of defensive communication. Clearly, the frequency, intensity and duration of the defensive communication patterns affect the scale of the consequences that ensue.

LISTENING IS THE FIRST ACT OF COMMUNICATION

Listening is an act of respect, not only for the person of another but also for his/her feelings, beliefs and values, no matter how contrary they may be to your own ways. Respect does not equal agreement with, but it does mean accepting that each person is entitled to have and to express his/her own viewpoint once the beliefs expressed are not a threat to the well-being of others. Naturally, if this is true for another, it is also true for you.

As in all our desirable dealings with others — love, respect, care, consideration — listening starts with self. Ironically, there are few people who know how to listen to self and, as a result, active listening to another is all too uncommon. The central tenet of this book is that each manager needs to know self and from that solid base of knowledge of self, to know employees. There is no more powerful way of knowing self than through listening to what goes on within you in feeling, thought and dreams, and listening to what goes on when you are relating to another. Everything we feel, imagine, think, dream, say and do, whether silently within ourselves or expressed outwardly to another, is a revelation of how well we know ourselves and of the extent to which we are manifesting our true potential. In practical terms, this means sitting with ourselves and noting, in particular, the feelings and thoughts that reveal at any one moment where we are and what specific responses might be required.

At the physical level, for example, fatigue is a common experience among many managers, but is often unmarked and unresponded to because the manager is not in tune with what is happening to his energy. All sorts of difficulties can arise from this non-listening to physical symptoms, e.g. irritability, impatience, susceptibility to colds and flus and lack of efficiency.

At the emotional level, managers can experience fear of failure, threat of criticism, dependence on success, anger at lack of appreciation but, owing to the most powerful defensive behaviour of all — denial — do not pick up on these emotions and so do not find resolution of the issues that are crying out to be heard. Listening in to our emotions lets us know whether we are in a state of welfare or in a state of emergency. A welfare state reveals emotions such as joy, love, excitement, enthusiasm, confidence, creativity, power, sureness. In an emergency state we feel emotions such as anger, sadness, depression, fear, threat, jealousy, loneliness. Welfare emotions give us the green light to reach out, take risks, be productive, take initiative, inspire others. Emergency feelings are the red light that warns us to stop and see what is happening and determine what responses are needed to resolve the emergency.

Such constructive responses to your emotions — welfare or emergency — will deepen your sense of self, increase your sense of empowerment and result in a more effective management of self and others. When emergency emotions are not heeded, the consequences can be devastating for the manager's own and others' physical and emotional welfare and, inevitably, the welfare of the organisation. Many workers know the kind of manager who comes to work day after day carrying major emotional baggage and, as a result, creating difficult work relationships. Unfortunately, this manager is not known to self and listening to self needs to be his first act of resolving his inner and outer difficulties.

When this does not happen, it is incumbent on the work organisation to constructively challenge the manager's defensive ways. When the manager does not respond to the challenge, the organisation cannot afford to allow his defensive actions to continue to be a source of threat to the well-being of other members of the workplace. Serious questions need to be asked and serious decisions made so that the organisation shows how well it is listening to the needs of its employees.

LISTENING TO EMPLOYEES

What emerges in our words reveals much about how we see ourselves, others and work. Managers would do well to be attentive to the words of their employees and also to their non-verbal accompaniments. Of course, there is some truth in the saying that actions always speak louder than words. Hence the need to observe that employees follow through on what they say. Sometimes it is the case that actions can do a good job of covering up an underlying reality that is a threat to the welfare of self or another. For example, you can be 'killed by an act of kindness' or freedom can be taken from you by the overprotective actions of another. It is the wise manager who is alert to such phenomena.

Managers need to pay particular heed to what the individual employee says about self, colleagues and work. For example, the staff member who continually puts self down, elevates colleagues and expresses hate for his/her work, deadens the group dynamic and lowers productivity. Similarly, the employee who is cynical, sarcastic, constantly complaining or who reacts aggressively to directives, presents a serious challenge to a manager. Again, the frequency, intensity and duration of the verbal defensive behaviours are important considerations and will inform the kind of confrontation that the manager will make. Such confrontation springs from a place of concern for the individual employee's welfare, the welfare of his/her colleagues and the effectiveness of the organisation.

The wise manager ensures that what he is confronting are specific verbal behaviours that are a source of threat to the work ethos. He must not in any way personalise the employee's defensive behaviours, he must ensure that the person of the worker is respected and that he is specific in the requests he makes of him/her. For example: 'I am concerned to have witnessed your verbal aggression towards your colleagues and am requesting you to reflect on and take responsibility for your own behaviour with them.' Following the confrontation, the manager will engage in 'uninterrupted listening', so that the employee feels that his/her side of the story is actively listened to and understood.

To understand any behaviour means to get below, to get under the 'stand' that the particular distressing behaviour is making. Only the employee can bring the manager to that place of understanding and this is more likely to happen when active uninterrupted listening is present. The manager who attempts to judge the situation and give advice is unlikely to create progress with the employee who is troubled. It is best that the manager creates the interpersonal safety that provides opportunity for the employee to come to his/her own understanding of a behaviour and to determine what needs to happen for the situation to be resolved. Certainly, the manager will be prepared to encourage and support these realisations on the part of the worker and is advised to set the date and time in the near future for a review of progress. It is crucial that such follow-up be carried through because defensive behaviours are like old soldiers — they die hard.

In the attempt to actively listen to employees, a manager may encounter several blocks:

- □ non-listening through distraction
- □ interference from 'my agenda'
- □ judgement of what is being said
- □ anxiety about what is being said
- □ advice-giving
- □ moralising.

Non-listening is a common experience where we find ourselves attending to issues going on in our own heads rather than to what the other person is saying. A manager may have an underlying attitude that what employees have to say does not really matter and so he lets them 'rabbit on' as much as they like to give the impression that they are being listened to, but he holds the view that, in the final analysis, 'it is what I decide that counts!' The manager who believes employees do not spot such pretence is hugely naïve and will find that his non-listening will add considerably to the conflict. The manager will get back from employees what he is giving out — falsity.

A frequent block to effective listening is interference from our own agenda. A manager may find himself preoccupied with what he wants to say himself and not at all listening to the employee's side of things. At the first available opportunity he comes in like a shot with what he wants and effectively sabotages the communication process. Of course, the manager is entitled to his views, but he needs to listen with his ears and eyes to the employee and be open to the possibility that his views may be altered when he allows himself to see all sides of the situation. When the manager cannot listen because he is following his own agenda, this usually results in employees not voicing their agendas and no progress can be made on anyone's agenda.

If the manager finds himself internally judging what the employee is saying, he has stopped listening; a disrespectful and unequal situation that the employee will intuit very quickly. For example, when a manager covertly judges the worker for what he/she is saying as 'a fool' or 'a know-all' or 'irresponsible', he will give no consideration to what the employee is saying and may well start a secret agenda to get rid of this employee as soon as possible. Clearly, no real relationship exists between the manager and this employee and, inevitably, the circular reaction will be for the employee to judge the manager in return. No progress is now possible.

When a manager feels anxious, it is very difficult for him to listen to others. He will be much more focused on coping with and covering up his anxiety and the other person will likely spot his vulnerability and realise that such a person is not in any secure position to listen to his/her needs. Some employees may defensively attempt to exploit what they perceive as this manager's 'weakness' and push through either covertly or overtly their own agendas. The precise source of the manager's anxiety is known only to himself, but the more common possibilities are: lack of confidence, dependence on how others see him, fear of conflict, fear of failure, poor level of competence and compulsion to please others.

A common block to active listening is the tendency to give advice. Advice-giving, though often well-intentioned, blocks listening, makes it unsafe for the employee to continue to speak and, effectively, is an act of superiority on the part of the manager. Wisdom involves supporting the employee to come to his/her own realisation of the sources of conflict and his/her own decisions about what needs to happen to resolve the situation. Such belief in the employee on the part of the manager boosts the worker's self-esteem and enhances the relationship between employee and manager; all of which bodes well for the organisation.

A further block to listening is moralising, where the manager decides the rightness or wrongness of what the employee is saying and shows scant understanding of the underlying sources and intention. In this case, the manager has stopped listening to the employee's story and is listening to his own notions of right and wrong. Such a response leads, and wisely so, to the employee drying up and retreating from openness with the manager, and communication now returns to a familiar defensive place.

When a manager finds himself blocked in listening in any of these ways, his challenge and his responsibility is to enquire into the sources of the blocks.

WHEN EMPLOYEES DO NOT LISTEN

Non-listening by employees poses quite a challenge to managers because it affects the work atmosphere and adversely affects productivity. The manager needs to be aware of particular employees who do not listen; these can be identified in formal and informal meetings and in non-compliance with directives. The reasons for not listening will be different for each employee; it helps when managers remind themselves that each employee hears him or doesn't hear him in a different way.

There are two key observations a manager needs to make before confronting an instance of non-listening:

- Is the non-listening generalised to all staff members, or specific to the manager, or to one or two colleagues?
- Is the non-listening generalised or specific to a specific circumstance?

Some employees may have difficulty with people in authority and defensively 'switch off' in their company. Another employee may feel intimidated by a colleague and close down in his/her company.

When an employee's non-listening is specific to the manager, then there is a call for confrontation between the manager and the employee in private. When non-listening is generalised — the employee does not listen to anybody — then the issue is more serious and the manager may need the support and involvement of the human relations department. In some work situations cliques of workers are created and listening occurs only for the grievances that have fuelled the creation of that clique. In order to address the adverse effects on the work ethos that this kind of non-listening causes, a major review of staff relationship, values, traditions, management style and reward practices is required. When the non-listening occurs in the presence of a particular work colleague, the manager may have a bullying situation to resolve.

The manager seeks to discover if the non-listening occurs only in specific situations; if so the resolution will be sought therein. It may emerge, for example, that non-listening is more common in formal group settings than in a one-to-one situation or in informal group situations. A crucial question for the manager to explore is what issues are being verbalised when the non-listening occurs. Observation here may reveal that certain work issues, e.g. technical issues, co-operation with others, deadlines, being asked for an opinion, are a source of threat to a particular worker and his/her defence is to refuse to hear. Observation may reveal non-listening at staff meetings to discuss social outings or staff parties as a result of the threat experienced by employees who feel that they do not belong to, or who are uncomfortable in, the company of others. When it is a specific topic that leads to non-listening, resolution is more straightforward.

Consideration of the 'when' of non-listening may reveal that it is the time of day or it is a busy time or a time of fatigue that explains why an individual employee is not in a position to listen.

DEFENSIVE VS. OPEN COMMUNICATION

Effectively, any communication that operates from the outside in is defensive in nature and blocks individual, interpersonal and organisational progress. Out-in communication places the responsibility for your actions on to others, and when those others do not conform to your needs or expectations you are likely to blame them or blame self. Either silently or verbally, the manager who blames others will see those who have not measured up to expectations as 'worthless', 'undependable', 'lazy', or 'thick'. This process is known as projection. The manager who blames self when things go wrong tells himself either covertly or overtly, 'I'm stupid', 'I'm useless', 'no good', 'out of my depth', 'in the wrong job'. This process is known as introjection. Whether introjecting or projecting, the manager is cleverly defending himself against criticism, judgement or ridicule.

By introjecting ('I'm useless') he takes the sting out of any possible criticism by blaming himself first. The blaming of self is defensive behaviour and is not the same as taking mature and open responsibility for your actions. On the contrary, the self-blame blocks him from taking ownership of his actions; it invites some kind of sympathy perhaps, but not the open confrontation that is required for progress. Further difficulties with the defensive response of introjection are that the manager is further away from any sense of his true potential and is not engaged in solving the problem. This manager needs to reflect deeply on his self-blaming and self-critical behaviour so that he may recover the real potential that lies behind his defensive screen. Depending on the frequency, intensity and duration of his introjective communication pattern, he may require professional help with the reflection and realisation work that he needs so much to do.

The manager who engages in projection poses a sizeable threat to the emotional, intellectual and social welfare of employees. There need to be back-up structures and resources for employees to resort to when faced with the aggressive verbal behaviours of this manager. It is true that the intention of the projective communication pattern is to reduce the possibility of the manager being held responsible for the failures encountered. Furthermore, it is not the direct intention of the manager to threaten the well-being of the employees and the work organisation; nevertheless, that is precisely what happens. Such a situation would not be endured for long by employees who have a strong sense of self and who have effective ways available to them within the workplace for confronting the manager's defensive behaviours. Sadly, such maturity among individuals and organisations is rare.

Out-in communication can take several forms but, no matter what form it takes, it invites reflection to the point of realisation of what aspects of self lie hidden underneath the defence and to active expression of those hidden qualities. The defensive communication also invites the organisation to question its policies regarding its dealings with its employees.

An effective way of examining out-in communication patterns is along one dimension of direct-indirect messages and a second dimension of clear-masked messages. Using these two dimensions, it is possible to identify three different forms of defensive communication:

□ indirect and clear
□ direct and unclear
□ indirect and unclear.

Discovery by a manager of any of these patterns in his communication invites him to move towards in-out communication which, of course, is direct and clear.

The manager who engages in indirect and clear communication tends to have a moderate degree of self-esteem — hence his ability to be clear — but finds direct confrontation difficult. The challenge for this manager is to realise more fully his sense of worthiness, equality with others and his right to be different so that he may have the internal, strong foundation that enables him to directly confront the person who is engaging in defensive behaviour or even, simply, make a request. The source of this manager's defensive means of communication lies in childhood years when it was not safe, physically, emotionally or socially to directly confront a parent, teacher or other significant adult on unmet needs or distressing behaviours. While the source lies in early life, the manager needs now as an adult to find and express his power with others. Until he resolves these childhood issues, he will subconsciously continue to deliver his message using the indirect-clear mode:

- 'People should take more responsibility for time-keeping' (no direct addressing of the particular individuals who are frequently late)
- 'We need to increase our output levels' (failing to target the individuals who are not pulling their weight)
- 'There appears to be a notion around here that people can come and go as they please without first consulting me.'

In the indirect-clear message the manager avoids facing the persons whose behaviour requires confrontation. The hope is that the individuals concerned will get the message without the manager having to face him/her directly.

The most common form of defensive communication made is the direct and unclear message. The vulnerability that lies behind this type of communication is, 'I find it too threatening to ask clearly for what I want.' The vulnerability leads the manager to find some way of getting his needs met without ever having to face the threat of rejection. The source of such a pattern of communication lies in early childhood years, when punishment, criticism, ridicule, dismissal and non-listening were the kind of responses that followed the expression of needs. The child finds a masked means of communication that lessens the threat – 'if I never say clearly what I want, then I can't be rejected' – but the underlying hope is that the person targeted will read between the lines and see what the child wants.

The manager who engages in the direct and unclear mode of communication can pile up problems for himself. Employees will know to whom he is speaking but will have no clear notion of what his needs, expectations and directions are and, while there will be some employees who will decipher the masked messages, the mass of employees will take matters at face value.

- □ 'John, the sun is high in the sky' (to a staff member arriving late).
- □ 'Mary, nose to the grindstone today!'
- □ 'As a staff I would like us to pull together more.'
- □ 'Michael, I was looking for you at half past eleven.'

In the above messages the manager is masking the real issues:

- □ 'John, I need you to be at your desk at 9.00 a.m.'
- □ 'Mary, I need this report to be completed today. Are you in a position to finish it?'
- □ 'I'm concerned that our production figures have fallen by 10 per cent and I need us to raise that issue at this meeting.'
- □ 'Michael, your coffee break is fifteen minutes and no longer than that.'

The above direct and clear messages lead to a stronger likelihood of progress than the masked ways of delivering those messages. The challenge for the manager is not to attempt to change the way he communicates but to discover the underlying issues that he needs to resolve within himself. In confronting those inner matters he will come spontaneously to be direct and clear in his communication. Behaviour always has a purpose and any attempt to extinguish or replace a response without discovering its meaning and intention will not work.

The most defensive mode of communication is where the manager neither clearly addresses the person nor the issue on hand. This manager's sense of self is very poor and he has learned not to trust the person or the behaviour of another. The source of the defensive communication lies in early childhood experiences of a highly neglectful nature, where neither the self nor the behaviour of the child was cherished. When you have been hurt to such an extent, then the defensive walls have to be very powerful. Comparisons, sarcasm and defensive communication are the more common forms of the indirect and unclear defensive mode of communication. The aim is to eliminate the possibility of further very painful experiences of rejection: 'If I don't speak to you directly and I don't tell you what I need, then you can't reject me or neglect me.'

The manager who carries within him the emotional baggage of a profound sense of unworthiness is not in a position to manage others, but if he is in such a role, then he can wreak havoc on staff members and create a profoundly disturbing work ethos. When aggression accompanies his communications, great threat to others is present. It is as if he were subconsciously re-enacting his own experiences as a child and with the hope that somebody will notice and take responsibility for the tragedy that has happened. This is a sad situation for all concerned and requires the urgent attention of the work organisation since the manager is too highly defended to be able to see the problem.

Examples of aggressive, indirect and unclear messages are:

- □ 'What kind of a fuck-up is this?'
- □ 'People don't know their ass from their elbow around here.'
- □ 'A monkey could do what this job requires.'
- □ 'Everybody is just out to get what they want for themselves.'

The above messages blame others but there is no clue to what precisely this manager needs and to whom his messages are directed.

Within the dimensions of clear-unclear, direct-masked, particular defensive messages can be further described as judgemental, controlling, superior, inferior, certain, manipulative, and neutral. Each of these types of message is protective in the sense that the manager who employs them attempts to control employees and pass the responsibility for his mistakes, failures and needs on to them. The manager (or employee) who discovers these defensive messages in his communication with others needs to see that discovery as a challenge to understand the underlying unresolved issues within himself and to set about freeing himself of his fears.

Judgemental: 'You're lazy; 'You're inefficient.'

Controlling: 'You do what I say'; 'You're not here to think for yourself.'

Superior: 'I know what's best for you'; 'What would you know about this topic?'

Certain: 'This is the only way to do this'; 'What I'm saying is correct.'

Manipulative: 'Do this for me and I'll see you right'; 'Don't let me down. I'm depending on you.'

Inferior: 'John, what would I know about that?'; 'Mary, I'm
                 not in a place to make a decision on that.'
Neutral: 'We can all feel upset at times'; 'What are you
                 getting angry about?'

In these examples the manager reveals very little of himself and
speaks mostly of 'you'. The manager who is secure within himself
will always speak for himself ('I' messages) and will allow employees
to speak for themselves. Furthermore, his communication will be
clear, leaving the employee in no doubt about what he is saying or
requesting.

If the manager were to resolve his inner fears, the above
examples would read as follows:

Non-judgemental: 'Jane, I need you to increase your work speed';
                 'James, I need more attention to detail in your work.'
Permissive: 'I would like to hear your opinion on those
                 schedules I've prepared'; 'I would appreciate your
                 thoughts and ideas on improving staff relationships.'
Equal: 'Mary, I'm quite sure you can come to your own
                 decisions on what needs to happen with those staff
                 members under your supervision who are frequently
                 late coming to work'; 'Connor, I'd love to hear your
                 ideas on new marketing strategies.'
Tentative: 'You have heard my views on how best to respond to
                 bullying but these are not cast in stone'; 'Helen, my
                 memory of the last staff meeting is as I've outlined
                 and I hear that you see it differently.'
Open: 'Sara, I'm wondering would you work late this
                 evening to finish this report?'; 'Susan, I'm stuck on
                 how to proceed here and I require your help and
                 expertise.'

Confident: 'Dan, my knowledge of this new technology is solid, but I'm still learning'; 'Seán, I'd like to give this matter consideration and I'll be back to you tomorrow with a definite decision.'

Empathic: 'John, I understand your resentment about not being consulted'; 'Sara, tell me more about what is making you feel so angry.'

The above mature ways of communicating are direct (person or persons are directly addressed) and clear (there is no confusion about what the manager is saying). Such communication creates a positive work ethos and ensures that the three 'r's of an effective workplace — respect, recognition and just reward for a fair day's work — are more likely to be met. The more each individual in the organisation works to know self, be separate and independent of others and become free of fears, the greater the benefit to the organisation. Introspection is an essential exercise to an effective and efficient work (or any other) organisation, but it is a behaviour from which many individuals, managers and organisations shrink.

CHAPTER 9

THE CHALLENGE OF CONFLICT

NO ESCAPE FROM CONFLICT

Conflict is intrinsic to living; without it, no progress towards self-realisation, effective management and organisational maturity is possible. Understanding the true nature of conflict is central to conflict resolution. Conflict is neither right nor wrong; it is what it is — an invitation to deepen maturity. The manager who says, 'I don't experience any conflict', is in a place of denial. This is a sad situation for all concerned and requires the urgent attention of the work organisation because the manager is too highly defended to be able to see the problem. It may be that the manager hates conflict or sees it as a threat to his status position and so does not allow it to manifest itself or ignores its manifestations. Much conflict lies hidden behind walls of fear of expressing what is true, but because conflict is hidden does not mean it is not present. What the manager needs to realise is that a blocked need affects the work culture and productivity, and it is his job to find ways of removing the block so that progress can flow within the organisation. This managerial task is never-ending.

Conflict emerges when there is an expressed or non-expressed tension around a blocked need or right. The block can be within oneself or can be external. For example, a manager may feel tense around his legitimate need for staff to arrive on time for work. On the one hand, it could be said that his need for punctuality is being externally blocked by staff members' tardiness. It could equally be said that the block lies inside himself, because how is it that he has not strongly voiced his need and taken due action with those staff members who do not co-operate? Possibilities abound to explain his passivity: a need to be liked by staff; the fear of conflict; the fear of bringing attention to his own lack of punctuality; the fear of being bullied by staff; the fear of being labelled.

Most conflict situations demand exploration of what is happening within each of the conflicting parties, what is happening between them, and the organisational context. In the example of conflict given above, there needs to be exploration of the organisational culture around time-keeping, the structures, if any, present to promote punctuality and the sanctions available to the manager for persistent lateness. These are important explorations, because the answers determine the possible responses available to the manager in dealing with the poor time-keeping.

When the block to action lies within the manager, there are deeper issues for him to resolve before he is ready to act on the time-keeping issue. When the block is outside him, and he does not perceive the staff members' lateness as being a threat to his sense of self, he is more likely to confront the issue in an open, mature manner.

Another example of conflict is where a staff member experiences a block to his/her right to respect. Once again, the tension arises around the blocked need, but the staff member is likely to confront the untenable situation only when he/she possesses a deep respect for self and carries that through to his/her relationships with others, whether in or out of work. Passivity is common among employees and it means that unmet needs that badly require to be expressed get buried in a swamp of silence.

The reasons why a worker might be slow to express and take definite action on an unmet need lie both within and without the person. For example, a worker who is being poorly paid and feels tension around that injustice may, within, feel unworthy to receive a raise and, without, suffer ridicule and aggression were he/she to voice his/her need. The creation of a safe environment by managers is crucial so that, at least, workers who experience tension around a blocked right or need may have the external support to voice their concern. In some cases, no matter how much a manager creates a safe climate for openness, the worker may still find it very difficult to take the risk of being assertive. In such a situation, the manager is best to hold the boundaries around his rights and needs, while at the same time encouraging, supporting and, perhaps, suggesting a direction for the staff member to go in search of the answer to what makes it so threatening for him/her to say what lies within.

Some workers never complain, but that does not mean that they do not experience tension around blocked needs. These workers may even rationalise that they love their jobs, even though for those looking from the outside in, their position is not at all enviable. While it is the responsibility of each individual employee to look after self, many workers are light years away from such maturity. Like individuals, organisations, particularly in the person of the manager, have a responsibility to show due care and to create opportunities for the enablement of their workers. Sadly, organisations too are often light years away from mature leadership. In such a situation where the worker, the manager and the organisation operate from defence, great neglect can occur.

Conflict is the fuel that propels individuals and work organisations along the road to fulfilment of needs and a realisation of potential. It is in the interests of all, especially of managers, to embrace conflict as an opportunity for deepening the well-being of self, staff and the organisation. It is in the interests of the organisation to provide structures and supports for managers to effectively respond to conflict. The process of conflict-resolution is never-ending, but the more a mature response to conflict is present, the more quickly will conflicts be resolved.

BLOCKED NEEDS ARE WHAT CONFLICT IS ALL ABOUT

Tension can arise around any need that is blocked: physical, sexual, emotional, intellectual, behavioural, social, creative and spiritual. It is the business of managers to know what needs are more likely to be blocked within the work-setting and to set about meeting those needs. It is also the manager's responsibility to enable workers to express their grievances so that a positive work ethos prevails. The manager who is in possession of self will take on these tasks automatically, whereas the manager who does not know self will be reluctant to take on these responsibilities.

Certainly, some progress has been achieved in the workplace in terms of the physical and sexual rights of workers. There are strict laws around physical work safety, and sexual harassment is now taken seriously. It is in the realm of emotional, intellectual, social, behavioural and creative needs that many workers and, indeed, managers themselves, experience dissatisfaction. Dissatisfaction in these behavioural domains is often expressed in 'don'ts'.

EMOTIONAL

- ☐ don't humiliate me
- ☐ don't embarrass me
- ☐ don't dismiss what I feel
- ☐ don't ridicule my emotions
- ☐ don't be aggressive
- ☐ don't be hostile
- ☐ don't be flattering
- ☐ don't say one thing but mean another

INTELLECTUAL

- ☐ don't put me down
- ☐ don't label me
- ☐ don't compare my work to another's
- ☐ don't over-reward success
- ☐ don't punish failure
- ☐ don't be sarcastic
- ☐ don't be cynical
- ☐ don't confuse knowledge with intelligence

SOCIAL

- ☐ don't ignore my presence
- ☐ don't ignore my absence
- ☐ don't dismiss my presence
- ☐ don't put me down in front of others
- ☐ don't shout at me in public (or in private)
- ☐ don't compare me to another
- ☐ don't look down your nose at me
- ☐ don't treat me as inferior

BEHAVIOURAL

- ☐ don't tell me I'm not capable of learning
- ☐ don't ridicule my work efforts
- ☐ don't make a song and dance about mistakes I make
- ☐ don't put me on a pedestal because I meet targets
- ☐ don't expect too much of me too soon
- ☐ don't mock what I do
- ☐ don't make more of my work in front of others
- ☐ don't use my achievements to boost your own career

CREATIVE

- □ don't steal my ideas for your own progress
- □ don't belittle my suggestions
- □ don't rubbish my ideas
- □ don't pretend that you don't see my creativity
- □ don't overpraise my initiatives
- □ don't deprive me of opportunities to demonstrate my unique giftedness and potential

When employees voice their blocked needs in such terms, they are effectively passing the responsibility for their needs on to the managers and the work organisation. It is far more powerful to express a blocked need in the form of an 'I' statement, so that there is no doubt about where the ultimate responsibility for the meeting of a blocked need lies. However, it is the wise manager and organisation that recognises that the meeting of workers' needs is basic to a positive work ethos and the maximisation of productivity.

EMOTIONAL

- □ 'I deserve respect at all times'
- □ 'I wish to be treated with dignity'
- □ 'I'm requesting direct and clear communication'
- □ 'I do not respond to being harassed'
- □ 'I wish for realness and authenticity in our contact'
- □ 'I wish to be heard'
- □ 'When difficulties arise, I believe politeness goes a long way towards resolution'

INTELLECTUAL

- □ 'I'm requesting that my intelligence be affirmed'
- □ 'Expressing belief in my potential helps'
- □ 'I want you please to see failure as an opportunity for progress'
- □ 'I want you please to see success as an opportunity for progress'
- □ 'I have my own unique way of seeing and doing things'
- □ 'I would like you to provide opportunities for me to learn more'

SOCIAL

- □ 'I wish for my individuality to be recognised'
- □ 'I have no wish to be like anyone else'
- □ 'I want you to please acknowledge my presence'
- □ 'I want you to please notice my absence'
- □ 'I want you to treat me as an equal'
- □ 'I need you to relate to me in a manner worthy of my dignity'

CREATIVE

- □ 'I wish for opportunities to express my creativity'
- □ 'It helps when initiatives I make are acknowledged'
- □ 'I welcome your interest in and support for my educational and career progress'
- □ 'Credit where credit is due is only fair'
- □ 'I will assert publicly my role in a creative initiative should you [the manager] choose to ignore or dilute it'

Whether blocked needs are unexpressed or expressed in terms of 'don'ts' or in more powerful 'I messages' it is the responsibility of managers to acknowledge the needs of employees and to be aware when such needs are not being met. It makes the manager's job considerably easier when employees voice their grievances in open, respectful and responsible ways.

BLOCKS TO THE EXPRESSION OF CONFLICT

Whether or not conflict gets expressed in an open way is a by-product of the level of safety that exists. The level of safety is greatly reduced where one or more of the following factors are present:

☐ oppression
☐ competition between needs
☐ fear of speaking the truth
☐ suspension of needs.

Oppression is an external force that makes it highly risky for an individual to voice his/her tension around blocked needs. Given that a high proportion of workers experience some form of bullying in the workplace, it is clear that oppression is a common source of conflict. Oppression is a protective means that a manager or organisation can employ to control workers to meet the needs of the organisation without any consideration of the rights of workers. The style of management is dominating, controlling, bullying, rigid, heartless and product-driven. In this culture, only the needs of the organisation count; it would not only be dangerous for a worker to express a grievance, it would also be threatening for a manager to go against such a coercive work system.

Where there is competition of needs, generally speaking the productivity needs of the organisation are valued by management more highly than, say, the employees' need for a family life to be taken into account. Similarly, in a situation where a particular manager is highly ambitious, the request of a staff member for some time off may threaten the manager's ambitions and so he is unlikely to accede to the employee's request. The more the requests of employees are refused, the more tension will build up around blocked needs.

One of our most common fears is the fear of being real, of saying what needs to be said; this fear arises from previous experiences that have shown how punishing it is to express a need. Such experiences originate in the family, continue in school and can be reinforced in the workplace that employs fear as a weapon. The fear of being real means that many needs go unexpressed in the workplace. Tension will arise around those blocked needs and may manifest itself indirectly through, for example, high absenteeism, sickness, aggression, low motivation, little initiative, perfectionism, or manager-pleasing behaviour.

There is no doubt that many workers suspend the expression of their needs out of a sense of unworthiness or out of past experiences of neglect, whereby parents and other adults were not responsive to their expressed needs. Not opening your mouth becomes a clever protection against anybody ever getting the opportunity of not hearing or of neglecting you again.

Whatever the blocks to expression of conflict, the job of the manager is to create the relationship with the worker that will make it safe for him/her to name his blocked need and the tension he/she experiences around it. Managers can be in a position to respond in this mature way only when they recognise and act upon the sources of their own inner and outer conflicts.

HOW CONFLICT MANIFESTS ITSELF

There are many ways in which conflict can defensively manifest itself; the more obvious ways being argument, aggression, uncooperativeness, emotional withdrawal and the development of cliques among the workforce. Obviously, the way conflict manifests itself will have a large influence on how a manager responds, particularly a manager who tends either to be on the defensive or the offensive. Even the mature manager may struggle to hold his equilibrium in the face of some of the more challenging ways in which conflict can reveal itself.

Open expression of conflict around a blocked need, which leaves the manager in no doubt about what precisely the staff member is revealing, is a rare phenomenon. Managers modelling direct and clear expression of their own needs can pave the way for employees to do likewise.

An open expression of conflict takes the form of an 'I' message that spells out how you feel and what you need. For example, 'I'm disappointed that my commitment to my work is rarely acknowledged and I would like to receive feedback much more frequently.'

It is a sad fact that the blocked needs of most employees emerge in protective rather than open ways. The reason why conflict is manifested in protective ways may be within the person or in the external environment. When the source of these protective ways is externally located in the shape of an unsafe work environment, there is much that a manager can directly do to remove the threats to realness and authenticity on the part of the worker. When the source of the defensiveness is internal to the employees in the shape of a poor sense of self, an addiction to what others think, or a fear of rejection, there is little a manager can directly do. However, in treating such employees with respect, showing belief in them and encouraging them to take on challenges, the manager may indirectly influence the staff members to reflect on their internal blocks and seek the help and support needed to free themselves of these inner restrictions.

Protective ways of manifesting conflict may be:

- non-verbal
- projective
- introjective.

The manager needs to understand that manifesting conflicts in protective ways is not a weakness, but a clever subconscious means of reducing the risk of further occurrences of previous experiences of being hurt, put down, embarrassed or rejected. Sadly, experience has taught the person in defence that speaking the truth directly leads to the triggering of protective responses on the part of others, with little chance of the conflict issues being heard, not to mind being resolved. But conflict never rests easily and so it finds other ways of revealing itself. The ingenuity of the protective ways is that they either make life very difficult for the other (let us say the manager) and for the organisation, or they make life very difficult for self. The subconscious hope is that such upset will draw attention to the unexpressed or masked conflicts and that support will be created for direct and clear expression.

Some examples of non-verbal protective ways of expressing conflict among employees include avoidance of contact with the manager, avoidance of eye contact, being frequently absent, being sick, being rarely on time for work, leaving work early or 'on the dot', overworking, constantly pleasing 'the boss', being clumsy, over-cautious in doing an activity, working late, coming into the office during off times.

Projective ways of manifesting conflict can be the bane of a manager's life. Examples are: aggression, refusal to co-operate, rudeness, constant whining, forever complaining, bullying, rigidity, hostility, gossiping, doing the least for the most money, non-listening, superiority, dismissiveness. Managers need to make sure that such responses are not part of their own managerial repertoire; otherwise, any attempt to confront others about such behaviour will not ring true.

Introjective ways of masking conflict can be particularly threatening to a manager who does not cope very well with emotional upset. Examples are frequent crying bouts, being easily upset, personalising any feedback, feeling put upon, blaming self for anything that goes wrong, being passive at staff meetings, saying 'yes' to all demands, being perfectionist.

Introjective ways of manifesting conflict centre on putting the pressure on self in the hope that somebody will see how difficult life is for you and will come to your rescue. The subconscious cleverness for the worker who introjects conflict is that he/she takes no risk. On the other hand, projective responses around conflict are designed to put pressure on the manager and the organisation in the hope that they will rescue the worker who is in distress. Once again the risk is put over on the other. It is in this sense that the masking of conflict by projective or introjective or non-verbal means has the same purpose — to pass the buck of responsibility on to the other. Only when individual employees or managers come into possession of their own presence will they then be able, directly and clearly, to express their dissatisfactions and blocked needs.

THE MANAGER'S DILEMMA

What is a manager to do in a situation where a staff member expresses a need for 'sympathy leave', but the manager himself is anxious to meet a deadline and needs this worker to stay in his/her job and the organisation is shouting in the manager's ear about falling revenue? This dilemma can be resolved only by the manager listening to and valuing the needs of the individual worker, his own needs and the needs of the organisation. When the needs of one of the parties are considered less worthy of attention, the inevitable consequence is a heightening of tension around the blocked need, leading to all sorts of other conflicts. Sometimes the very fact that an expressed need has been listened to and valued is what is most important.

In the scenario described above the manager could request the worker to stay on until the deadline is met and then take his/her sympathy leave. Another possibility is that he requests a colleague of the worker to do overtime to facilitate the sympathy leave. For every blocked need there is an infinity of solutions. As for the falling revenue, the manager could arrange a meeting with those who are complaining and suggest a brainstorming session for solutions.

Whenever anybody in the workplace shows tension around a blocked need, checking his own inner response is a first step for the manager because there is a likelihood that an employee's dissatisfaction will trigger a reaction within the manager. The possibility then is that a competition of needs emerges and the manager may have difficulty in maintaining a fair response. For example, if a worker reports to the manager that he/she is being bullied by a work colleague and the manager himself feels intimidated by that same employee, then his inner response to the complaint may be one where he feels threatened by the prospect of having to confront the bullying behaviour.

Unless the manager comes to understand the source of his fear and takes action to resolve it, he is not in a mature position to respond effectively to the complaint of bullying. More than likely what transpires is that he will take no action. His passivity will result in him letting himself down, as well as the worker who is being bullied, the work organisation and, indeed, the employee who is engaging in the bullying behaviour. The consequences of the non-resolution of the conflict issue are that an unsafe, threatening work ethos is allowed to continue, which in turn will adversely affect staff morale and productivity. The worker who is being bullied may well move on to another job and the company loses a conscientious and responsible worker.

The manager also needs to keep close watch on his overt responses to an expressed conflict. Clearly, when he reacts, rather than proacts, the conflict issue will be exacerbated rather than resolved. Of course, the manager who is effective will often spot conflicts that require redressing before the complaint is made. The earlier tensions around work issues are identified, the easier it is to arrive at solutions. Sadly, in some workplaces, dissatisfactions are allowed to fester, even over several years, before some major crisis erupts that highlights the unresolved conflicts.

When a manager does not constructively respond to conflict, there needs to be back-up structures in place whereby an employee who is troubled can bypass the manager and find another to listen to his/her troubles. Many organisations lack such resources, and the result is that they pile up problems for themselves.

CHAPTER 10

MANAGING CONFLICT

CONFLICT AS A CREATIVE FORCE

Whether a person is in an open or a defensive place, conflict always creates the opportunity for progress within and between the conflicting parties. This is true of personal, interpersonal, occupational, community, religious and political conflict. Whether or not conflict is seen as opportunity is determined by the level of self-possession and maturity of each individual party to the conflict. Managers who do not know themselves or their workers are unlikely to welcome conflict for its creative potential; on the contrary, as illustrated in chapter nine, conflict will be perceived as a threat and all sorts of defensive manoeuvres will emerge to reduce or remove the threat.

The purpose of conflict is to alert us to the challenges that need to be taken on so that an increased level of personal, interpersonal and organisational well-being is achieved. The frequency, intensity and duration of the conflict are important barometers of the depth and seriousness of the underlying triggers. It is not what is shown but what lies hidden that needs to be the target of conflict resolution. However, what is shown is a window in to what lies hidden, to its depth and duration. When defensiveness is what is shown, it is this that, more often than not, becomes the focus of attention, rather than the underlying trigger. Such a focus is in itself a defensive ploy since it reduces the threat of having to face the real issues that demand confrontation. When openness is present, the focus of attention is on understanding the manifestations of conflict and seeking to discover those aspects of self that are frightening to show but are now demanding to be shown.

The manager who knows self and his employees seizes the potential opportunities that conflict brings to the organisation. Whether the primary source of the conflict lies within himself, within one of the employees, in the relationship between himself and staff, between staff members themselves, or with the structures, traditions and values of the organisation, he is willing to relentlessly explore blocks to progress. He does not doubt that the conflict that has surfaced will deepen the well-being of the workplace. He does not believe that it is best to 'let sleeping dogs lie' but he realises that unresolved conflict can eat into the heart of an organisation and cause great distress to its members. He is not willing to jeopardise his own or others' well-being and if the organisation does not back up his pursuit of conflict resolution, he will challenge its intransigence. If the organisation does not positively respond, he is likely to seek employment elsewhere. It is often the case that when such a mature manager leaves the organisation, an exodus of other employees will follow.

While it is an essential management task to respond effectively to expressed conflict, an added skill is to detect conflicts that are unexpressed or are strongly masked. The real issue will not be at all clear when conflict is manifested in *non-verbal ways* (for example, absenteeism, arriving late, having extended coffee breaks, sighing), or is *projected* (for example, 'you're impossible to work for', 'no one listens here', 'nobody cares', 'this place just takes me for granted') or *introjected* (for example, 'I'm to blame for anything that goes wrong', 'I'm just not up to it', 'I never get anything right'). In such cases, it is up to the manager to find ways of enabling the employee to openly express the hidden conflict issues so that the process of conflict resolution can be initiated.

There are many subtle and powerful ways for employees to mask tension around unmet needs. These protective strategies begin early in childhood when expressed needs may have been ignored, dismissed, punished, harshly rejected, ridiculed or laughed at. At that early age, children learn to hide their unmet needs behind powerful defensive walls and, unless the hurts have been resolved, these protective ways become more reinforced over time. The manager who wants to know his workers will be on the lookout for these protective strategies.

There is no suggestion here that the manager takes on a therapeutic role; it is not his job to resolve the personal and interpersonal problems of employees. However, it is his job to ensure that the personal and interpersonal problems of employees do not become barriers to the creation of positive working relationships and to productivity. Certainly, a manager needs to show care and concern around the out-of-work problems of staff members, but his primary management task is to nurture and enable each staff member to work to his/her potential, to contribute positively to staff morale and to co-operate with the needs of the organisation. The wise manager realises the necessity for the workplace to be considerate of the person, marriage, family and community, but not to the extent that the needs of the organisation are jeopardised or lessened. It is quite a managerial balancing act to respond to the needs both of the organisation and employees, but that is where his expertise needs to lie.

CREATING SAFETY FOR CONFLICT TO BE EXPRESSED

Safety in the workplace has tended to focus on physical safety and, to a lesser extent, on sexual safety. Certainly each employee has the right to both physical and sexual safety and any threat to or violation of these boundaries cannot but be viewed seriously by the manager and the organisation. It is also crucial that individual employees feel safe enough to bring any violation to the attention of the manager or human relations department. When it is the manager who has been the source of the violation, then direct and confidential access to a named member of the organisation is necessary.

What workplaces are only beginning to appreciate is that an enormous amount of emotional and intellectual hurting occurs between staff members, between managers and staff and between owners and managers.

In order to ensure that conflict does not remain unexpressed or masked, it is the manager's responsibility to create the safe environment that will allow mature expression of blocked needs. Emotional and intellectual safety are created by ensuring that all interactions, particularly between manager and employees, are of a nature that enhances relationship, and enables and elevates the employee's sense of self. There needs to be an absence of ridicule, aggression, cajoling, 'put downs', comparisons, pressure to perform, over-emphasis on deadlines, labelling, cynicism, sarcasm – any interaction that lessens the presence of an employee. On the other hand, the manager ensures the presence of valuing the individuality of the person, affection, support, belief in, encouragement, compassion, affirmation, appreciation, consultation, recognition, understanding – behaviours that enhance relationship and the individual employee's sense of self.

Behavioural safety is created by ensuring that failure and success are treated as intrinsic to and equal partners in the pursuit of progress; of course this safety can be created only by the manager whose own behaviour is guided by this belief. The acceptance of failure and success as having the same purpose, which is to set the next challenge, goes a long way to ensuring progress in relationships, creativity and productivity. The support and encouragement of considered risk-taking is another factor that contributes to behavioural safety. Managers need also to be wary of comparing one employee's attainments with those of another; such comparisons reduce the possibility of risk-taking on the part of the person being compared and put pressure to perform on the other person. Far too many employees go for the average, for what can be achieved with minimum effort, because of experiences of the punishment of failure and the over-rewarding of success.

One thing a manager can be assured of is that each worker has an innate drive for his/her unique social presence to be celebrated. The common complaint of anonymity in the workplace suggests that many managers are not aware that the appreciation and affirmation of each employee's presence are essential aspects of creating social safety in the workplace. Social safety makes it much more likely that individual workers will reveal any tensions they have around particular blocked needs.

A further type of safety that managers are advised to seek to integrate is creative safety. Each worker brings a unique giftedness and limitless potential to the workplace and it is the wise manager who identifies and encourages such creativity.

UNDERSTANDING THE SIGNS OF CONFLICT

Matters are rarely as they appear; in the case of conflict, when it is unexpressed or manifested in defensive or deeply masked ways, the task becomes one of uncovering what lies unsaid beneath the presenting behaviour. Only when an individual can directly and clearly express what his/her needs are can you take the declaration at face value that that is what the conflict is about and that that is what needs to be resolved. For example, the manager who feels tension around an employee's silence at meetings and who makes a direct and clear request — 'John, I would like to hear your opinion on issues raised during these planning meetings'— is much more likely to have his conflict with the worker resolved in a straightforward manner because his need is out in the open. The manager who is in a defensive place might say nothing, or gossip about the employee to colleagues, or be sarcastic ('John, you're so vocal at meetings, you have to learn to be quieter'), or show verbal aggression ('Nobody seems to have an opinion around here').

In this case, before the conflict can be resolved, the first task is to uncover what the manager actually requires in the situation. If both manager and employee are in a place of defence, there is nobody now available to do the job of uncovering the hidden need. It is only when at least one of the parties moves into an open and real place and actively attempts to understand what blocked needs are involved in the situation that there is some chance of progress.

It is important for the manager to understand that, even though he may make a direct and clear request of a worker concerning a blocked need, there is no guarantee that the worker will be in a position to respond positively. In the example above, the manager's request for the staff member to verbally contribute to planning meetings represents the manager's attempt to resolve his own conflict issue. However, the staff member's silence may have nothing directly to do with willingness to participate. His/her silence may be masking a deep inferiority complex or a fear of being bullied or a fear of failure or a fear of not appearing intelligent. When the manager finds that the staff member does not respond to his reasonable request, he now needs to don his cap of understanding and create the opportunities for the staff member to realise and resolve the true origin of his/her defensive silent behaviour.

In his attempts to understand the employee's underlying issue, it can be useful for the manager to ask the 'w' questions concerning the presenting behaviour:

□   with whom does it arise?
□   where does it arise?
□   when does it arise?
□   what is happening when it arises?
□   why does it arise?

Answers to the first four questions can be gleaned through systematic observation. In the example being discussed, observation might, for example, show:

□   silence occurs with other section leaders and the manager (the who?)
□   in the manager's office (the where?)
□   at the weekly planning meeting (the when?)
□   plans for the coming week are being discussed (the what?)

The 'why' question can be answered only by the person concerned, and considerable safety at all levels is required for the staff member to be forthcoming in this regard. If the manager asks head on, 'Why do you have difficulties talking at planning meetings?' he needs to be prepared for more silence. It would be wise for the manager to consider the nature and strength of his relationship with this employee, and should he notice any shortcomings in this essential aspect of his managing, it would be best to work on enhancing the relationship rather than directly confronting the silent behaviour. There is also the option of suggesting that the person talk to somebody else within (or, indeed, outside) the organisation if he/she does not feel ready to open up to the manager himself.

When the worker does not respond to any of the opportunities presented, the manager needs to resort to back-up support within the organisation that will strongly challenge the person either to take action or move on from his/her position. It cannot be allowed that the problems of any employee continue indefinitely to threaten staff morale or the execution of work responsibilities and productivity. Whatever the nature of the confrontation, it is crucial that it is done with respect and confidentiality. One thing is sure: defensive responses always have a story behind them. When the manager discovers the truth of what lies hidden behind the other's difficult stand, his response is likely to be one of compassion rather than condemnation.

A manager in a large organisation once approached me about the high level of staff absenteeism. A year before, they had decided to tackle the problem, and had invited the staff members who had shown high absenteeism to meet a panel of managers. Each staff member was informed of the frequency of his/her absenteeism and the amount of time lost to the organisation over the previous year. The employee was also informed of the financial cost to the organisation and the very real disruption of customer care. The result of these meetings was that absenteeism doubled. The manager who approached me asked the question, 'why did that happen?' The answer was that the organisation fell into the trap of seeing absenteeism as the problem and confused the organisation's need for work attendance with the workers' defensive behaviour of being absent. There had been no attempt to follow any of the 'w' questions, and the most important question, 'why', was not asked at all. Subsequently, it emerged that the 'why' was serious bullying by a number of key managers.

MANAGING CONFLICT FROM THE OUTSIDE IN

The manager who fears conflict will experience considerable personal and professional threat when it appears. Rather than embracing conflict for the creative opportunities it presents, he will resort to all sorts of defensive manoeuvres to offset the threat. When a manager reacts defensively to conflict situations, it is inevitable that the conflict will continue to worsen until some major crisis wakes up somebody else in the organisation to the untenable situation. Because the aim of the conflict is to establish well-being, it necessarily escalates until such well-being is achieved.

There can be many different defensive reactions to the onset of conflict, the most common being to blame the workers or the organisation. Such blaming can be overt or covert, and may be outwardly expressed or internally voiced as follows:

- □ 'the staff are useless'
- □ 'the staff don't care'
- □ 'this organisation is impossible to work for'
- □ 'people just don't want to co-operate'
- □ 'workers are only out for themselves'
- □ 'the world markets are against us'
- □ 'staff always find something to complain about'
- □ 'what else could you expect from this motley lot?'

The purpose of the above projections is to deflect attention from the manager. This manager is likely to have a subconscious fear of failure, of not being good enough, of 'being found out' to be not up to his job, or to have an addiction to success, so that any conflict is perceived as a threat to his perfectionism. Whatever the cause, the intention of the manager's blaming responses is to ensure that he is not held responsible for the conflict. His defensive reactions may drive the conflict underground (which would suit him) or they may visibly increase the conflict (which would be highly threatening for him). Unless some employee goes above the manager and reports the unresolved conflict, it is unlikely that any resolution will emerge.

A manager who fears conflict can also resort to ignoring its existence by burying his head in the sand. Such managers often 'go missing' or 'hide' in their offices or 'go sick' when conflicts arise. Their unavailability and approachability intensify during times of conflict.

Another typical defensive attempt to deal with conflict is for the manager to blame self:

- □ 'I'm useless'
- □ 'I should never have taken this job'
- □ 'I'm in way above my head here'
- □ 'What else could I have expected for myself?'
- □ 'I'm no good with people'
- □ 'I'm a disaster'
- □ 'I've let everyone down'

It may appear that the manager is owning at least some responsibility for the conflict situation when he blames himself. However, there is no attempt here to analyse the nature, source and possible resolutions to the crisis. In blaming self, the manager emotionally and intellectually cripples himself and effectively blocks any mature and responsible proaction. The intention of the blaming of self is similar to the blaming of others — to offset the possibility of employees or the organisation holding him responsible for the crisis. Self-blame usually results in people feeling sorry for the manager and not wanting to pile further woes on to his shoulders. Subconsciously, self-blame is a clever strategy.

Unless somebody in the organisation can see through the ploy, the crisis situation will have been flown in vain.

The manager who is a perfectionist and who believes he has to be in charge of everything becomes highly threatened when conflict comes to the surface. Because his own inner conflict issues are so deeply hidden, he is unlikely to pick up on the unexpressed conflicts of employees or of the organisation, though these are just as potent as those that are obviously present. His defensive response to evident conflict will be to redouble his own work efforts in the hope this will bring about resolution. However, the consequences of this are that he becomes more highly stressed and puts more pressure on workers with his relentless checking of their work. Indeed, the very source of the conflict may be his obsessive behaviours, and the intensifying of these will only serve to increase the tensions around the blocked needs of the workers. This manager is not even remotely effective at problem-solving and he is at high risk of occupational burnout.

MANAGING CONFLICT FROM THE INSIDE OUT

The mature manager knows that whether it lies within or without, unresolved conflict blocks the flow of energy, drive, ambition, commitment, co-operation and creativity which is required for the attainment of individual, group and organisational goals. The wise manager knows that conflict resolution is central to his role as leader and that that challenge is unending. He realises the creative potential of conflict and he is not afraid to open it. In confronting conflict, he is aware that he needs to do so with heart and head. The heart response creates the necessary emotional, intellectual and social safety and positive regard for the person involved and the head response provides the energy, drive, definiteness, intelligence and creativity to find solutions. Both forces – heart and head — are central to the resolution of conflicts. Solutions that are only head-driven fall flat quite quickly; so too do those that are only heart-driven.

It is fascinating that the feminine approach is called 'soft' by those who are frightened to explore that side of self, while the masculine approach is viewed as 'hard' by those frightened of that aspect of self. The manager who is open to expressing both aspects of his humanity knows that it is the combination of 'softness' and 'hardness' that propels the resolution of conflict.

A core aspect of resolving conflict from the inside out is the manager's ability to maintain separateness from the conflict issues, whether or not these directly involve himself. Once a manager personalises the conflict issue, he goes into defensiveness and now can no longer effectively manage conflict resolution; on the contrary, he exacerbates the conflict situation. Certainly staff members will sense his defensiveness and will retreat into defensiveness themselves.

A not infrequent conflict issue is the complaint by a staff member of a manager's verbal harassment and intimidation. Considerable progress in conflict resolution has already been made when the individual staff member has found the safety, either within self or in the workplace, or both, to voice his/her complaint. The manager who personalises the complaint is likely to react by labelling the employee as 'weak', 'hypersensitive' or 'a cry-baby'. Such a response is a further act of intimidation and the staff member will now need to go to back-up resources to get his/her complaint heard.

The mature manager is well aware that we can all slip into defensive responses and this is true for himself as well as for others. His immediate response to the complaint will be to actively listen to and assure the staff member that he is willing to apologise for any hurt caused and wants to set matters right for all future interactions. He will want to know all the facts of the situation and will pay particular attention to the non-verbal and emotional expressions that accompany the telling of the violated need. He will also enrol the staff member's help in how he can best meet his/her needs and will arrange follow-up meetings to monitor progress. He will be determined to learn from the situation and to reflect more regularly on the aspect of his behaviour that led to the demeaning of the other person.

Separateness means that the manager hears the complaint not as being about him, but as being one hundred per cent about the person making the complaint. Many people find the notion of separateness confusing and say, 'surely if the manager has been verbally harassing and intimidating the employee, then the complaint is about him.' It is not for employees to define the manager's issue; the responsibility for them is to define their own blocked needs around him. If the manager hears the complaint as being about him, then his attention is drawn to himself and is drawn away from the staff member — he effectively stops listening. The staff member's complaint is about his/her reaction to the manager's behaviour, and it is this reaction that needs to be the manager's focus so that he can take the necessary steps to meet the staff member's violated needs.

At another time, when on his own, the manager does need to reflect on his behaviour and take action to resolve his own issues. However, these are two separate processes and must not become enmeshed. Separateness means allowing each person to define their own truth around the blocked need and neither party can assume to know what is happening inside the other person.

Whether identifying or attempting to resolve conflict, the wise manager brings all his in-out qualities to the challenge, particularly

those that enhance relationships, as well as his capacity to understand and his belief that co-operation brings solutions. He verbally
reinforces the staff member's openness and shows belief in the skill
and responsibility that he/she brings to the conflict-resolution. At
all times the manager stays in possession of his own self, ensures
that all interactions are worthy of the dignity of the staff member
who is distressed, and keeps sight of his overall vision for the
organisation.

Conflict resolution involves a high level of maturity, a knowledge of self, a respect for others and an understanding of human
behaviour. This is a tall order for any manager. However, if you
have the ambition to take on a leadership role, an essential
prerequisite is that you learn to be in charge of self. Leaders can
bring others only to the same level of maturity and development
they have attained themselves. Work organisations have a
responsibility to select managers who possess a strong sense of self,
a belief in their potential, and a deep regard for, and belief in,
others. Ongoing opportunities for personal, interpersonal and
professional development are best provided by the work organisation. When these opportunities are not present, the manager
himself needs to request such resources or pursue those challenges
himself. To date, organisations and managers have not prioritised
emotional and social maturity as being an essential prerequisite to
effective management, but there are clear signs of a shift towards
a management style that both nurtures and enables.

STAGES OF CONFLICT RESOLUTION

Each and every conflict needs and deserves a unique response. A
manager who applies the same problem-solving techniques to
different conflict situations is likely to miss the unique source and
intention of a particular crisis. The best that a manager can do is

to have some guidelines on how to respond to a conflict, but be sure that he applies those guidelines in a way that matches the uniqueness of the presenting conflict.

The essential step in conflict resolution is *identifying* the conflict and *understanding* that the presenting challenging behaviours are not the problem in themselves, but are masking the real issue that requires attention. It is common for managers to assume that, for example, absenteeism, poor time-keeping, a low productivity rate, bullying, passivity, gossiping or non-cooperation are the problems to be tackled. However, the reality is that these difficult behaviours are masking the real issues that the employees are not in a position to directly and clearly express. Getting information on the who, where, when, what and why of the defensive behaviours is likely to uncover what lies behind the presenting challenging behaviours.

Possible hidden issues underlying the aforementioned challenging behaviours are: bullying (absenteeism), family or marital problems (poor time-keeping), fear of failure (bullying), low sense of self (passivity), wanting to be liked (gossiping) and fear of not being good enough (non-cooperation).

Conflict-resolution often falls down at this stage of identifying the real issue that requires attention. The position in the organisation of the person who identifies the conflict may determine whether or not any further action is taken. For example, when a rank-and-file worker identifies the conflict matter, it may stay with him/her. However, when somebody higher up the responsibility ladder identifies the challenge, then the next stage in conflict-resolution is more likely to be pursued.

Communicating openly with those who are directly involved is clearly the best option in conflict resolution. However, what can often happen is that the conflict matter is talked about with an uninvolved party or is gossiped about to friends outside the work environment. Talking to others may provide support and guidance, but if it is for some other purpose, the involvement of others blocks a resolution of the matter. The manager needs to get his facts correct and even then be tentative about his conclusions when he is talking about the conflict. It is essential that he talks from a position of 'I' and avoids the defensive temptation of 'you' messages.

When agreement is reached on the cause and intention of the conflict responses, the next stage is to look for possible solutions. The exploration of these requires emotional, intellectual, social and creative safety if those present are spontaneously to suggest possible ways forward. Such safeties need to be at both a verbal and non-verbal level. The sigh, the grunt, the eyes being raised to the ceiling, the tut-tutting, the wink, the disapproving facial expression, the table-tapping are but some of the non-verbal ways of extinguishing creative risk-taking. Brainstorming is the most exciting stage of conflict resolution, and when there is emotional and intellectual safety it can mark the beginning of improved staff relationships.

Probably the most difficult step in conflict resolution is the choosing of a particular intervention from the options suggested. It can help proceedings to consider which option will most benefit the staff member who is most at risk or, indeed, the manager himself. When there is a difference in opinion regarding which option to choose, then agreement to try a particular option for a period of time can be suggested, with the agreement that the other favoured solution will be adopted should the option chosen not prove effective.

CHAPTER 11

ORGANISATIONAL SUPPORT FOR EFFECTIVE MANAGEMENT

THE WORK CULTURE AND MANAGEMENT

It is unlikely that an organisation will have a manager whose style of management runs contrary to the culture of the organisation. It is important to remember that a work organisation is a collective of individuals, but when a particular type of culture evolves it implies that each member of the collective is singing from the same hymn sheet and dare not introduce a different hymn. Changing the culture of an organisation is no mean task. Change is more possible from the top down than from the bottom up, but a highly organised and mature workforce can ring the changes. There appears to be a growing awareness at corporate level of the need to change work cultures to being more considerate of the person, of relationships and of family life, and for managers to possess more relationship skills alongside their technical skills.

The organisation as an entity has no power to change anything; it is individuals who transform an organisation. But the radical manager requires back-up within the collective of individuals that makes up the organisation, particularly those individuals who hold posts of responsibility higher up the hierarchy of power.

Organisational well-being is possible, especially when there is commitment on the part of each individual within the organisation, top-down and bottom-up, to creating a work environment that is fundamentally caring and dynamic. However, like any other social system, each member brings a certain level of emotional baggage to the work culture and, unless there is an acknowledgement of that reality, any progress towards wellness is unlikely. Leaders have a special part to play in realising, understanding and resolving their own vulnerability and providing opportunities for others to transform themselves. In the smaller and family-managed work settings, the owner or manager has a pivotal role to play and will largely determine the vibrancy, well-being, individuality and creativity of the work culture. There is no doubt that this owner or manager has to look to self first before he dares take on the task of confronting others on aspects of their behaviour that pose a threat to the well-being of fellow workers and to productivity targets. In a small organisation, the owner or manager is in a powerful position to create not only the back-up responses to any neglect of a worker's welfare, but also to create the structures and procedures that enshrine the caring approach of the organisation.

In a larger organisation, the manager can be caught between a rock and a hard place. In particular, middle managers can be in the very difficult position, whereby the top layer of management pressures them from the top down and the lower management level pressures them from the bottom up. It is no surprise that it is this level of management that exhibits the highest stress and illness responses. Unless the middle manager has the support, structures and procedures that reinforce a mature management style, it will be very difficult for him to exert his wisdom. Even when there is tangible support from top to middle management, if lower-rank positive responses are not present, the manager will find it difficult to get the largest group of organisational members to row in with policy and cultural changes.

Enrolling the co-operation of workers is an essential management task. Management credibility is determined not by the language of 'informed' management, but by the actions of the manager; workers will not respond to words when these are not grounded in action.

A culture statement that encapsulates the essence of the work culture is a starting point in good management practice. Such a statement needs to emphasise several important organisational aspirations:

- people matter
- couple relationships matter
- family matters
- relationships between management and workers matter
- relationships between workers matter
- relationships between the organisation and staff matter
- belief in the potential of each organisational member matters
- back-up procedures to deal with neglect matter
- work responsibilities matter
- the aims of the organisation matter
- management style matters
- communication matters
- productivity matters
- creativity matters
- achievements matter
- sociability matters
- vulnerability matters
- community matters
- fairness and justice matter
- spirituality matters
- ongoing career development matters
- ongoing educational development matters

The prioritising of people has not been a common feature of work organisations. Politically, socially, educationally and occupationally, it is unwise in any way to lessen or demean a person's presence. The defensive consequences of employees feeling anonymous, feeling that productivity matters more than their welfare are easily detectable in such common responses as burn-out, absenteeism, sickness, staff turnover, poor ethos, low staff morale, extreme competitiveness, worker cliques, passivity, aggression, job dissatisfaction and work sabotage. It may be difficult to define precisely a work ethos, but you can sense its nature and its effects on employees. There are some workplaces where the workers literally become sick at the thought of going to work and, on the other hand, there are those work organisations where the positive ethos is palpable when you enter the place.

There is a reluctance on the part of some organisations to embrace the concept of valuing the individual presence of each staff member. I remember one person at a seminar who, dismissive of the concept, exclaimed that 'workers have to conform, and that's the way it is'. I responded that I felt a far more desirable response is co-operation and that one of the primary tasks of managers and supervisors is to enrol co-operation. Co-operation involves a decision by a staff member to go along with a particular work practice and this freedom to respond increases a worker's motivation and commitment. Conformity is something that is enforced and, accordingly, does not contribute to a healthy work ethos. There appears to be a fear — either conscious or unconscious — in political, religious, educational and work institutions of empowering their members as if, somehow, respect for the individual is going to trigger all sorts of rebellious responses! But, it is within work organisations where conformity is demanded and the organisation attempts to own and control the lives of its workers that a revolution is much more likely to occur.

In recent years I have encountered several large work organisations that have developed working principles along the lines of:
'we have to be better than anyone else'; 'we can always improve
on how we do things'; 'we should take pride in our achievements';
'people matter'. Sadly, placement at the end of the list of the
'people matter' principle strongly suggests that this value was
purely aspirational in nature, though it is movement of some kind.

On the face of it, the principle 'we have to be better than
anyone else' might seem reasonable in a competitive environment,
but one significant difficulty with it is the imperative of 'have to'.
'Have to's', 'must's', 'ought to's', 'should's', 'should not's' can
become a tyranny within a workplace and always declare an ethos
in which the product is more important than the person. The 'have
to be better than anyone else' also implies a reluctance to learn
from others, and an insularity that eventually may implode.
Certainly, there needs to be an assertion and a determination to do
business in a way that enables the organisation to be competitive,
but this needs to be coupled with an openness to learn from others
and the maturity to recognise and appreciate the accomplishments
of other organisations.

There is no difficulty with the principle that 'we can always
improve on how we do things'. Creativity is a requirement for the
survival and ongoing development of a work organisation, and its
absence leads to stagnation and ultimate failure in the market or
in the effective provision of a service.

Taking pride in achievements is a risky principle because 'pride
always takes a fall'. There is another more serious psychological
issue and that is that pride associates achievement with the
person, thereby creating an unhappy enmeshment between the
self and work performance.[1] Performance anxiety is the most

---

1. My book *Work and Worth, Take Back Your Life* fully explores this issue.

common fear and one that seriously threatens the person's physical and psycho-social well-being and can cripple risk-taking, autonomy and creativity. Praise of achievements is good practice when the praise is applied to the specific attainment, e.g. meeting a weekly turnover target or resolving a particular conflict issue.

If the manager communicates to employees that they are wonderful because they reach a production target, he is likely to foster a dependence culture where employees feel anonymous in terms of their person and sense that they are only valued for their 'good' behaviour. This eventually becomes counterproductive because employees will begin to detect the manipulation and know how quickly they can be toppled from their pedestals when they do not please the organisation. Employees deserve respect at all times for their person and recognition for their specific attainments. In order to maintain a wellness ethos, these two rights of employees need to be kept separate. Similarly, when it comes to talking with a worker on falling short on a particular attainment goal, the focus needs to be on the challenging behaviour, not the employee.

There are no 'bad', 'lazy', 'useless' employees, but there are certain bad, lazy, useless behaviours that threaten the goals of the organisation and that need to be challenged. Resolution comes much more quickly with mature communication which separates the person from the behaviour and maintains the integrity of the person while dealing with the difficult behaviour.

In considering the list of organisational aspirations identified above as being important in creating a mature, productive work culture, it is possible to distinguish six main categories of aspiration. These are concerned with:

□ workers' relationships outside the organisation
□ relationships within the organisation

- [ ] development of the organisation
- [ ] the selection of managers
- [ ] the enablement of employees
- [ ] the relationship between the organisation and the community.

It is the responsibility of the organisation to create the structures and procedures that will ensure that these are made real. Ultimately, it is the people who are at the top of the organisation who are the architects of the work ethos. It is their beliefs and aspirations that become embodied in the values, traditions, taboos, laws, beliefs and work practices of the organisation. The main target for change needs to be those people who hold the key decision-making power. Certainly, workers have their unions to ensure that their voice is heard in decision-making, but the decision-makers within the unions also strongly need to reflect on their own level of personal maturity.

In order positively to transform work organisations and trade unions, people in positions of power need to start with themselves. This is their responsibility. If they can bring a radically different point of view to their daily practice within the organisation, change will come about. Communication of the vision of 'one for all and all for one' to managers and rank-and-file workers and their unions is a crucial task for these leaders. When those with the decision-making power are in denial around an exploitative and defensive organisational ethos, as well as being non-reflective on their own level of maturity, the work organisation will be truly stuck in its defensive morass. Change, then, is only likely from the outside in and this is a much slower and more painful process.

An important question that needs to be tackled within the organisation is, how can those in positions of power be challenged to be accountable for their actions? Some mechanism is needed to ensure that leaders can be challenged on their beliefs, values and work practices. Those leaders who are mature will ensure that there are structures and procedures in place to address this issue. The more common situation is that those with decision-making power operate in ivory towers or in some faceless centralised location where access to them is well nigh impossible. However, grounds for optimism is the fact that now psychology is touching every aspect of life — family, religion, education, community, law, environment, politics, work. It is only a matter of time before the deeper understanding of human behaviour that is coming about will permeate the defensive walls of those who hold positions of power. In the meantime, each of us continues to have the responsibility to push for the kind of work environment that looks after our well-being and that is worthy of our dignity.

EMPLOYEES' RELATIONSHIPS OUTSIDE THE ORGANISATION

Clearly, the less emotional baggage and outside-work stress an employee brings to the workplace, the better for the organisation. Some emotional baggage is very evident — drug addiction, alcohol dependence, violence, aggression, extreme passivity, perfectionism. However, each person possesses some level of vulnerability. Workplaces have tended towards the attitude that employees 'should' leave their troubles outside the work entrance and while inside focus solely on their work responsibilities. This is not something that can be done to order, and laying down a 'should' about it, far from making it happen, is only going to exacerbate the stress and vulnerability that are present.

If leaders reflect on themselves, they will find that they too bring their emotional baggage and life stressors into their work roles. The mature approach is to accept this reality and, instead of trying to avoid it, rather strive to create the kind of work environment that will not heighten vulnerabilities and that will provide opportunities for their resolution. The establishment of policies and practices that are considerate of the person, family life and couple-relationship will lessen the impact of workers' life difficulties on their work performance. Respect for the person, and flexible working hours that recognise the demands of family life and the stresses and strains of two people living together, will go a long way towards ameliorating the strain individual workers may undergo.

The acknowledgement of their unique presence and giftedness in the workplace can often be a lifeline to vulnerable employees, particularly to those individuals who may be in or come from families and relationships where no such acknowledgement of their worth exists or existed. Indeed, the valuing of their person may be the very support they need in order to begin to find regard for self. Calling individuals by their preferred title, daily affirmation of their presence and concern about their absence are the interactions that need to be enshrined in the culture of the workplace. Family and couple relationship days, photographs of staff members on workplace walls, crèche facilities are further ways of acknowledging and valuing relationships outside the workplace. Flexible work hours to accommodate family needs can be a boon to family well-being.

There will be individual employees, managers (and, indeed, leaders) who are deeply troubled and are in need of long-term psycho-social professional help. Without jeopardising its own aims and objectives, and ensuring that the behaviours of those who are troubled do not threaten the well-being of other staff members, the organisation can offer assistance and encouragement to troubled employees to seek the help required to resolve deep difficulties. When these employees refuse the assistance offered, it needs to be put in no uncertain terms that those behaviours that are a source of threat to others and that are interfering with work responsibilities cannot be tolerated and they may be required to leave the organisation. It also has to be asserted that a reference for other employment will reflect the extent of their willingness to take responsibility for their vulnerabilities. Some employers breathe a sigh of relief when a worker who has been difficult chooses to leave, but it is not good practice to unreservedly recommend this person to another employer.

It is a sure thing that the workplace that is considerate of the person, family and couple-relationship will reap the benefits of loyalty, commitment, higher work motivation and higher productivity from the employees they treat with such care. Naturally, any caring situation is open to the possibility of exploitation, but the organisation's own care of itself will guard against this eventuality.

RELATIONSHIPS WITHIN THE ORGANISATION

A natural follow-on dimension of the manager's responsibility is to ensure that the relationships within the workplace are ones where care, respect, equality, fairness and openness are displayed and where there is direct and clear communication. This applies to the relationships between managers and workers, workers and workers, workers and clients, and the organisation and workers. Of course, an organisation *per se* cannot have a relationship with its workforce, but the values, structures, rules, regulations, back-up resources to deal with neglect, and career and educational opportunities, bear witness to the unseen figures of decision-making power that are at the heart of the foundation.

The organisation needs to have as its core philosophy respect for the individual and for the rights of all staff members to physical, sexual, emotional, intellectual, social, creative and spiritual safety.

Those with decision-making power need be aware that their managers and other employees take their cues from how they interact with them and with each other. The subconscious intelligence of such an identification process is that when I imitate those in positions of higher power, I may become their 'favourite' son or daughter. Identification can operate with either desirable or undesirable behaviours. When the leadership of the organisation displays mature responses, it is more likely that employees will also operate in a way that is true to themselves — behaviour which is far more beneficial to the organisation. It is also true that when leaders believe that power, wealth and status make them more important than others, a dark ethos will emerge in the organisation of which they are leaders.

While organisations are now obliged to have an anti-bullying policy that is clearly communicated to their members, the existence of a policy is no guarantee of physical, sexual, emotional, intellectual and social safety. It is the genuineness and conviction with which these policies are implemented that will determine whether or not employees report neglectful experiences. The organisation that truly wants its culture to be free of harassment between its members will also promote an anti-passivity policy. This organisation will strongly encourage its employees to be assertive on their needs, grievances and any neglect experienced. Rather than reports of incidents of neglect being seen as a weakness or whingeing, such acts will be strongly reinforced.

Furthermore, those staff members who do not speak up will be admonished for their passivity, which is not only an act of neglect of self, but of others and the organisation. The more staff members feel safe enough to speak out, the less likely it is that bullying and other kinds of neglect will occur. Such maturity is only beginning to occur in the workplace, since it is still largely the case that the person who blows the whistle on neglect is the one the organisation seeks to marginalise, rather than the staff member who perpetrated the neglect.

DEVELOPMENT OF THE ORGANISATION

Organisations are created to meet their own aims and objectives and, just as it is the responsibility of each worker to take responsibility for his/her own life, equally it is the responsibility of those who created the organisation to take responsibility for the purpose for which it was brought into being. Whatever the purpose of the organisation – be it profit, education, provision of health care, care of the environment, tax collection, social welfare – everything needs to be done to meet its ends, once there is no allegiance to the dangerous notion that 'the end justifies the means'. In order to effectively meet its objectives, those who hold the decision-making power in the organisation need to be aware that to ignore the person, the living circumstances and the vulnerabilities of employees, is to give rise to all kinds of defences that block the aims of the organisation.

In societies where there is poverty and high unemployment, the danger that workers will be exploited is very great. In so-called developed countries, where there is no longer abject and widespread poverty, and where little or no unemployment exists, there is less danger of exploitation because workers can move on to other work opportunities. Staff loyalty has now become a considerable challenge for organisations and has, in many cases, provided the motivating force for the emergence of person- and family-friendly companies. But kindness with a hidden agenda is quickly spotted by employees. It is those organisational leaders who genuinely care for their employees who reap the true benefits of staff loyalty, commitment and high performance.

Communication is the life-blood of organisations and bringing across the vision of what the organisation has been created for is a highly significant factor in meeting organisational needs. The employment of appropriately trained and experienced staff and the appointment of managers who are people-centred, who are dynamic and creative and who are effective communicators is paramount to organisational development. A clear vision of the aims and goals of the organisation needs to be directly and clearly communicated by those who have the decision-making power to the managers and supervisors who operate at the ground level with the employees. Many managers feel either marginalised in their role or too fearful to seek support or advice from the upper echelons of the organisation. Unavailability, unapproachability and the use of fear as a weapon to control managers are not only unworthy of organisational leaders but are counterproductive; and what is likely to emerge is discontent, low motivation or even sabotage.

Who challenges the defensive behaviours of those who hold the power to make major decisions is an important issue in terms of the well-being and progress of an organisation. The vision presented here is that those who hold the reins of power would continually reflect on their own level of maturity and continue to take appropriate action. Because the key issue is knowledge of self and others, it is truly incumbent on those who hold major organisational power to look first to themselves before they dare to take on the leadership of others. It appears that a demand for this kind of leadership is emerging from employee bodies, but it would be far more desirable that such a movement towards wisdom would come from leaders themselves rather than from the outside in. Trade unions have played, and continue to play, a crucial role in the identification and vindication of the rights of workers. However, unions themselves are also a collective of individuals with hierarchical levels of decision-making power and as for a work organisation, there is no guarantee that maturity, fairness and justice are integral to their practices. One of the most significant shortcomings of some unions is the lack of consideration of the rights of employers. Championing the rights of workers does not have to mean jeopardising the rights of the work organisation. Taking the responsibility to know self and others is as much a responsibility of union leaders right through their hierarchical system, as it is for the top people in work organisations.

There is no suggestion here that those with major decision-making power have to undergo psychoanalysis or psychotherapy — even though this would be no bad idea — but these individuals need to at least recognise how they relate to others, the effects of their attitudes and behaviour on the work ethos and the seeking of effective means of resolving their conflictual and defensive behaviours. Travelling this road of inner and outer wisdom will not only benefit the work organisation but will have a positive influence on their own individual physical and psycho-social well-being.

THE SELECTION OF MANAGERS

A vital organisational responsibility is the selection, monitoring, ongoing training and development of its managers. Technical skills are a *sine qua non* of effective management, but so is the requirement of human relations skills. Somehow, the latter skills have not been viewed as being as necessary or as difficult to acquire as the technical skills and experience needed to do a particular job. But, as far as managers are concerned, failure to take account of a lack of personal and interpersonal maturity is a serious, and ultimately costly, oversight on the part of a selection panel of an organisation. The fact that such managers are allowed to continue in their role is a further act of neglect by the organisation, not only of the workers and the workplace itself, but also of the manager.

Naturally, those who select the managers will be *au fait* with the particular technical skills required for the job, but it is also recommended that they know themselves and have considerable insight into human behaviour and, in particular, managerial behaviour. Unfortunately, this is often not the case, and the problems for the organisation often begin at this point where the required care has not been taken in the selection process.

The choice of manager is largely determined by the ethos of the organisation. For example, organisations that are militaristic and controlling in their ethos will select a manager who is authoritarian rather than authoritative. Many organisations that are service-oriented, particularly health and education, tend towards the team approach. However, many team-style organisations have not learned that a hierarchical (vertical) structure is counterproductive and that what is required is a horizontal structure with decisions being made at a team level (not by one of the professional team, which is often the case, particularly in medicine, psychiatry and education).

Some organisations seek to project the image of 'one big happy family', but in reality control is hierarchical, and the employee dare not have a life outside the organisation; not at all a happy family! There are some work cultures wherein people are treated like machines and others wherein their workers are treated like animals. It is clear that such organisations will not attract a manager who is self-possessed and who values others, and he will not be attractive to the organisation because the threat posed by him would be too great.

When those with the decision-making power do not reflect on the style of management operating within the organisation, there is little chance of change from within that organisation. Those leaders who do reflect will seek to employ managers who are technically skilled, person-centred, effective communicators, assertive, grounded and can manage from both the head and the heart.

THE ENABLEMENT OF EMPLOYEES

Belief in the potential of each employee is an essential aspect of person-centred management, as is, within reason, the provision of opportunities within or without the organisation to explore that potential. The prevailing attitude in many organisations is that some workers have little or no potential and it is pointless to have expectations for them that go beyond meeting their current job responsibilities. The danger with this attitude is that it becomes a self-fulfilling prophecy, unless the employee gets encouragement from elsewhere. Sometimes the organisation wants to hold on to certain employees and is threatened by the notion of their proceeding beyond their present level of functioning. This is a short-sighted approach which, because it does little for the self-esteem level of the employee will inevitably, affect his/her loyalty, commitment and work output. Employees may choose not to avail of the opportunities provided; their motivation may be elsewhere, but, nonetheless, they will recognise the support being offered and, as a result, are more likely to maintain their commitment and output.

It is the responsibility of the organisation to create opportunities for leaders, managers and employees in the areas of personal and interpersonal development. A contented and mature employee is a far more promising prospect than an employee who is plagued with insecurities, fears and inadequacies. Employee assistance programmes are now common but, once again, their effectiveness is determined by the level of maturity of those who are providing the service. Research has consistently shown, for example, that in psychotherapeutic or psychoanalytic practice, it is not the type of therapy that is the critical influence, but the level of maturity of the therapist. In-house programmes on staff relationships, communication, assertiveness, self-esteem, stress management, anti-bullying and anti-passivity will be of help to those employees who have some degree of insight into themselves and others.

Employees who are in denial or who are defensive around their insecurities and are resistant (out of fear of exposure) to courses or on being advised to go to a psycho-social professional pose a serious challenge to the organisation. In such cases, confrontation is required which is of a nature that demonstrates care, but also firmly lays down the needs of the organisation in terms of work responsibilities and staff relationships. Whilst taking full account of workers' rights, the organisation cannot allow any one employee to jeopardise the rights and needs of the organisation and its other members. Any trade union that supports such threats to an organisation needs to review its operational policies.

It is a good idea for the organisation to have a list of psycho-social professionals on whom they can call when needed. Word of mouth is still the best way of discovering the more effective practitioners from among those who are appropriately qualified and accredited. It is essential that no direct contact with the practitioner is ever made regarding an employee's progress, except on fitness to work; fitness, in this context, meaning physical, psychological and social readiness for work.

The organisation's attitude to human vulnerability will determine its response to the enablement of employees. There are organisations which show no tolerance of human vulnerability but, ironically, such intolerance is a vulnerability in itself and so it is the case of the immature leading the immature. Vulnerability is not a weakness; it is a defensive screen that individuals and collectives of individuals subconsciously form when any threat to their well-being is present. The greater the threat, the greater the vulnerability. To view vulnerability as a weakness is to miss an important opportunity to harness the intelligence and power that creates defensive behaviours in the interests of freeing self and achieving the greater good of the organisation and its members.

THE RELATIONSHIP BETWEEN THE ORGANISATION AND THE COMMUNITY

The work organisation has a responsibility to the community within which it resides, not least because it would be unwise to ignore the surrounding territory. Certainly, the workplace — no matter how big or small — needs to be considerate of the attractiveness and physical security of the environs it occupies. The workplace that is open to being part and parcel of the community and that makes available its facilities (for example, lecture theatre, crèche facilities, green spaces) to community groups is likely to be more accepted and, therefore, more effective. Employees may live in the local area and their loyalty to their workplace will certainly be influenced by the organisation's relationship with the community. A further consideration is that when employees take pride in their workplace's attractive environment and its positive relationship with the community, they are more likely to encourage others to work there, including their own offspring.

THE ORGANISATION'S CULTURE STATEMENT

It is wise for the organisation to set out clearly and openly the kind of culture it wants to promote. However, the organisation has to ensure that what it says is what it does; otherwise no allegiance to its aspirations is likely to emerge from employees. What follows here is an example of a culture statement that can be adapted to the size, nature, purpose and aims of the particular organisations.

Culture Statement

This organisation was formed for profit-making reasons. However, we realise that our most important asset is our employees and that care and respect for each individual comes first.

We recognise, too, that without attention, flexibility and kindness around the personal, family and couple needs of our employees, we do not create the positive ethos that is required for staff loyalty and commitment to our needs.

We are aware that some employees may have personal and interpersonal difficulties and, within reason, we are open to the provision of appropriate help for these individuals. We are also very definite that the troubled behaviours of an individual (or group) cannot be allowed to jeopardise the rights to physical, sexual, emotional, intellectual, social, creative and spiritual safety of other staff members or, indeed, our needs.

We are interested in the ongoing career and educational development of our employees and are willing to consider and support, financially and otherwise, the aspirations of individual staff members. We are committed to the development of a strong presence within, and an interactive positive relationship with, the community.

We well know that the nature of leadership is crucial to the positive ethos that is required and we have consciously employed managers and supervisors who operate a person-centred management approach. This approach emphasises respect and belief in regard to each employee and the mature carrying out of work and relationship responsibilities.

Structures are in place for any employee to express confidentially any grievances, and we are committed to the fair and just resolution of whatever conflict may arise. We particularly want to affirm the absolute necessity for employees and those having management and supervisory responsibilities to assert their rights, needs and any neglect experienced. We do not tolerate the neglect of anyone, no matter what the person's status or position within the organisation.

Hand in hand with the consideration of the welfare and development of its employees, the company is equally determined to remain focused on meeting its own objectives and requests the co-operation of all staff members in this aspiration.